Applying Old Stories to New Lives

Tina Durham

authorHOUSE®

AuthorHouse™
1663 Liberty Drive
Bloomington, IN 47403
www.authorhouse.com
Phone: 1-800-839-8640

First published by AuthorHouse   3/23/2011

ISBN: 978-1-4567-5564-5 (e)
ISBN: 978-1-4567-5563-8 (sc)

Library of Congress Control Number: 2011904793

Printed in the United States of America

Any people depicted in stock imagery provided by Thinkstock are models, and such images are being used for illustrative purposes only. Certain stock imagery © Thinkstock.

This book is printed on acid-free paper.

Because of the dynamic nature of the Internet, any web addresses or links contained in this book may have changed since publication and may no longer be valid. The views expressed in this work are solely those of the author and do not necessarily reflect the views of the publisher, and the publisher hereby disclaims any responsibility for them.

Preface

This book is based on my prayerful meditations on what the old stories must mean to us in the everyday present world. In our time, we have historians and scientist all running around attempting to demonstrate whether the stories are true or if they could even be accurate. The religious leaders always state that we use our faith with these stories in these times of faith questioning and proving, not be a "doubting Thomas" in these times. We do not have to see the scars or the proof, we believe because of the unseen.

The intent of this book is not to change the real meanings in the Bible, but to make us think about the simple parts. Relying on the old trait of finding meaning and symbolism in literature, I have examined these stories.

As you read the stories in scripture and the version of interpretation that I have found, ask yourself, what is God saying to you? Scripture is the love letter from a friend, God. He speaks to each of us differently and with different directions, these may not trigger the same thoughts in your understanding, but if they bring cause for you to examine the word, then I have been successful.

As you begin to read this book, be prepared to ask yourself questions.

Be prepared to listen to what God is telling you. So often we read a story and that is the story, we never revisit it. But the Bible is not like a regular book; it can be read over and over, each time revealing something more intriguing than the last.

The layout of this book is to first consider who we are, what our role is in this vast community of people. Then I move through a section imaging how we interact and learn to live in God's love and grace. Finally, I discuss some of our daily activities such as work, school, home ownership, and voting.

Walls Separate and
Divide and the Ceiling Limits

E ver read the church signs as you drive down the road? Ever wander if the person who posted the statement actually stood back and read the sign to check the message and tone?

It was Holy Week when I saw the most disturbing sign in a minute: "He died for your sins." I realize that in itself the statement is platonic; however, in my warped mind, the word "**your**" stood out. Really? Once we enter those wooden doors our sins are never more. I guess that church is special because my church is still full of people who need to have their sins forgiven, especially me. Ironically, the sign would have been more inviting and more believable if they had left the "y" out: "He died for our sins."

The first institution that God was established in was a tent. Today, all religions rely on beautiful buildings, churches, tabernacles, synagogues, cathedrals, mosques. Do you remember the tent revivals denominations used to have in summers? I remember how inspirational they were. There were no limits on God's movement from front to back, right to left, inside and outside.

> All who are skilled among you are to come and make everything the Lord has commanded: the tabernacle with its tent and its covering, clasps, frames, crossbars, posts and bases....And everyone who was willing and whose heart moved him came and brought an offering to the Lord for the work on the Tent of Meeting. Exodus 35: 10-11; Exodus 35: 21 (NIV)

The Lord commanded that the Israelites build a tent not a building. What is amazing about a tent tabernacle is that we cannot limit where God is assembled. He may be in one location one Sabbath and then another tribe the next Sabbath. This limited the power that the people covet for having God in one place. God knows us so well, that He wanted to establish the fact with us that He is every where and any where we are.

Institutes of religion have an uncanny ability to create an air of power and establishment. We establish the rules of who can join and the requirements of who can stay within the group. We post signs of discontent for those outside our building. We attempt to invite others, but our messages sound more judgmental than inviting. We have forgotten the tents of old, where people just met to celebrate and praise God.

It was amazing to listen to the voices; but today, you drive by an institution and the windows and doors are closed, no longer can you hear the celebration.

Yet, I want to push the edge of the box. I want to think further in where we may find true celebration with God: Outside in nature. Have you ever really stopped to listen to the sunrise outside the city limits? Have you ever really stopped to listen to the sunset outside the city limits? Everything in nature gives praise.

> Praise the Lord. Praise God in his sanctuary, praise him in his mighty heavens. Praise him for his acts of power, praise him for his surpassing greatness. Praise him with the sounding of the trumpet, praise him with the harp and lyre, praise him with tambourine and dancing, praise him with the strings and flute, praise him with clash of cymbals, praise him with resounding cymbals.

> Let everything that has breath praise the Lord. Praise
> the Lord. Psalm 150 (NIV)

For many years now, we have decided that family vacations were to center on observing nature. Traveling in a vehicle across the country is a perfect way to notice all the wonders of God's hands. You notice God in the mountains, valleys, beaches, flatlands, and canyons. You notice God in the various species, especially the really small and funny ones. You cannot look out into the Badlands then turn your back and look up into the Black hills without realizing there was a master plan. You cannot look into the Grand Canyon and not reflect of God's patience.

We are attracted to water. We will seek out waterfalls and watch the surf come in and go. The power of water is so remarkable. Everything on Earth needs water. Water the only true dichotomy on Earth. Too little water or too much water and every species and plant risks death. So my family drives out of our way to find water while on trips. We will hike for miles into unknown woods just to see a trickle of water or frozen falls.

Water constantly reminds me of my baptism. I was baptized in a river in southern Indiana; therefore, recall to that moment around running water is not difficult. The force of a waterfall, even a trickle, brings one to the realization of the cleansing power of God. It allows us to feel the sins washed from our souls.

> And now why do you wait? Rise and be baptized, and
> wash away your sins calling on his name. Acts 22:16
> (NIV)

Your head leans into the waterfalls, your back slowly slides in, and you adjust your legs under to stable yourself. Suddenly, the cold water rushes down through your hair, over your face, down your shoulders and the rest of your body. You hear nothing but the water rushing around your head. You are submerged in the power of water, the power of cleansing, the power of healing, and the power of God. You say to yourself in the name of the Father, Son, and Holy Ghost, and you are committed again, refocused, rejuvenated.

Water is not our only attraction; we have climbed the tops of mountains. Ironically, climbing the mountains are very similar to spiritual mountains. You walk forever up the hill, struggling, and every muscle tense and worn out; and at various times throughout the walk there are glimpses of beauty. Promising a reason to continue up the mountain, and when you reach the summit, there are no words to say. The feeling of relief, the feeling of accomplishment, the feeling of awe overwhelms you for a minute and you must sit and give praise.

> I will turn all my mountains into roads, and my highways
> will be raised up. Isaiah 49:11 (NIV)

We had hiked for over two hours and were just getting to the summit. My legs were exhausted from carrying the waters and snacks and all in the hackie-sack. I thought for sure I was just going to start falling down the mountain. We had watched so many people stop along the way and turn back, were we insane? There it was, one of the highest points in the Great Smokey Mountains. The fog was limiting some of the view to the north, but the other three directions were AWESOME. From the top of the mountain, so many facets come to life. You are small. In the whole realm of nature, people are small. Yes standing by an ocean gives one that feeling as well, but from up high, you see how small you are, just as God does. You look down but you cannot make out the difference between trees. At the top of the mountain, you do not see where you started, only where you can go from there.

I enjoy my church. I need to go to a place where it feels like family all around me. A place where everyone else is struggling on the road, looking as lost as a child in a mall without his or her parents, open to all. However, the closeness that I have felt with God has been in nature. His Spirit is not limited by walls; His Spirit is not contained by a ceiling. He moves me more in the quietness of His tabernacle than in ordained buildings.

Institutions of religion do not want to acknowledge this but what would be the point of God's first church being a traveling tent. What is the point in the New Testament when Jesus travels?

> For where two or three come together in my name, there
> am I with them. Matthew 18: 20

God is every where. We acknowledge it every time we sing praises. We honor His gift of nature in the teaching of the rainbow, birds singing, and birds not even falling without His knowledge. Yet, we build a building and lock ourselves inside and nature outside. We allow God to only enter through those that are there. We shut the windows and doors to not allow praises outside.

We set rules of who can come in and who can stay. We limit our God by not acknowledging Him outside. What if we all took our prayers outside? What if we all took our praises outside? What if we showed our kids God's hands at work? What if we looked into the Grand Canyon and saw His patience in work?

If you looked at His world in His eyes would you protect her more? If you respected His work in the world would you respect His work in you?

How powerful it is to look out at the sunrise or sunset and ask who did this. You hear the answer so peacefully, "I did." The colors that you view on a horizon illustrates that He is the most captivating artist. He creates colors that we still try to combine, but yet ours don't mesh into that perfection.

In the seasons, we learn the beauty in change and how to accept change. The spring brings new life, no argument, but have you ever noticed the number of different greens? We go to sleep one night, and the next day, life is there. We were shoveling snow, and now we are getting gas for our mowers. In an instant, God said "Awake" and nature did.

Everything is in perfect step. Summer brings full bloom and celebration for the life that has been awoken. Fall hazes its sleeping gas on nature, and God begins to sing the lullaby with the spectacular colors and wild movement of animals. He commands everything in perfect harmony to its place of preparation. Finally, He speaks, "Rest" and nature slows down to a sleepy winter. Yet, the colors are not gone. He does not leave life plain; He remains with greens from the evergreens, and blue in the streams and skies. Many of the most magnificent light shows are at winter evening, whether from the moon and the stars or the incandescent sunset.

He first asked to be a traveling God. He did not want us to limit Him behind walls and under ceilings. He has provided many examples of Him in nature. We must go seek Him out. We must learn to praise God with whoever is with us. Change in nature prepares us for change in our lives. If we believe that nature's changes are natural and in God's control, how can we doubt ours? How can we fear ours?

So as you prepare for your first adventure to God's tabernacle recall:

> I come to the garden alone, while the dew is still on the roses, and the voice I hear falling on my ear, the Son of God discloses.

And He walks with me and He talks with me, and He tells me I am His own; and the joy we share as we tarry there, none other has ever known.

Recognizing God

It was a typical Easter season that we were experiencing: The same stories that every Sunday talked about Jesus' appearance to the disciples after His crucifixion and resurrection. Then out of no where the question was asked, "Why didn't anyone recognize Him at the beginning, why only when He spoke?" What is the point that no one recognized Him? Every story in the Bible has a meaning, so why don't we talk much about the fact that no one recognized Him?

> At this, she turned around and saw Jesus standing there,
> but she did not realize that it was Jesus. "Woman," he
> said, "why are you crying?" Who is it you are looking
> for?" Thinking he was the gardener, she said, "Sir, if you
> have carried him away, tell me where you have put him,
> and I will get him." Jesus said to her, "Mary." She turned
> toward him and cried out Aramaic, "Rabboni!" (which
> means Teacher). John 20: 14 – 16 (NIV)

Some have taught, in past years, that the reason no one recognized Him at first was because He was in His Heavenly body. He was no longer in the man-form because He had risen from the grave. However, if you read the text she noticed Him as a gardener. Isn't that a human form?

This is not the only account of His people not recognizing Him, the road to Damascus is another example when the disciples were walking with a man and did not recognize him at first as Jesus. So what is up?

I believe some of the answer to the question is found in the beginning.

> So God created man in his own image, in the image of
> God he created him; male and female he created them.
> Genesis 1: 27 (NIV)

God created all humans in His image. Each of us possesses a unique part of God in our spirit. From the beginning, we have been set to recognize the God in each of us, but we keep looking at other physical traits that we cannot see God, and only when He speaks do we recognize Him.

The point that none of His followers knew Him on first encounter was because they were not prepared to see Him in others. He spent time reappearing to them in various forms to teach them and us that He is in everyone. Look for Him in the gardener or the stranger on the road. Look for Him in the person next door. Imagine that for a moment.

It is good for our faith to realize that Jesus would no longer be in the form that was hung on the cross or left in a tomb. If by some chance of luck the scientist or historians found a body and could prove that it was Jesus, then realizing that He was not recognized in that form by His disciples after His resurrection, gives us hope that He is no longer in that form.

It is stronger for our faith to realize that Jesus would be a gardener or stranger on the street.

I have this neighbor who has in plenty of times been extremely mean and hateful. As a matter of fact, this person has been over heard to have threatened my life. Rising from under the cross, I have had plenty of opportunities to see God over there. I have taken the time to shovel the walks, push them out of their drive, and rescue them in times of medical need. Each time I have reached out to assist them, I have seen God, not a mean neighbor. I have heard God in their voices of gratitude and relief. My faith has grown more not on my works, but by using God's eyes to see others.

Ever worked for that boss that everyone dreads? Had the reputation that the person is not easy to work for? I have and talk about looking deep and hard for a God light.

It was several weeks into the new job, when I felt that my back was going to break from being on the road so much. Every time I turned around we were doing something wrong and getting into trouble constantly. We would correct one issue, and another would arise from the solution. I felt as though a microscope was being used to watch my every move. Trust me under a microscope, every mistake can be seen, I mean let's face it; we examine molecules with these tools.

I kept trying to figure out what was the purpose. I kept trying to find perfection. I kept seeing God, only the judging God. I felt that this boss had died and become the gate keeper: Checking everyone's credentials at every stop.

In a meeting, it had finally made its appearance. The God light I had been searching for. This boss was not after perfection and was not judging anyone, this boss wanted success.

His master replied, "You wicked, lazy servant! So you knew that I harvest where I have not sown and gather where I have not scattered seed? Well then, you should have put my money on deposit with the bankers, so that when I returned I would have received it back with interest. Take the talent from him and give it to the one who has the ten talents. For everyone who has will be given more and he will have abundance. Whoever does not have, even what he has will be taken from him. Matthew 25: 26 – 29 (NIV)

The goal was to grow the program, help as many as possible. With this little group growth was expected and group control at the low level would be the foundation for the higher levels. The program grew and grew. Each student, regardless of race, gender, or age, was viewed as little God lights.

Consider how much our lives would be changed if we looked for the God lights in each and every person we met. We would not have road-rage, we would not have hunger, and we would not have people dying alone.

> People were bringing little children to Jesus to have him touch them, but he disciples rebuked them. When Jesus saw this, he was indignant. He said to them, "Let the little children come to me, and do not hinder them, for the kingdom of God belongs to such as these." Mark 10: 13 – 14 (NIV)

Jesus was indignant, angry, offended, insulted, and snubbed. If we are all in the image of God, and if the kingdom of God is for all of us, do we not need to accept each of us as a child? Do we not need to learn to greet each other as God lights?

He was insulted and snubbed because His disciples were pushing them away. In all His lessons, He was with the people we call undeserving. In every encounter that He had with people He greeted them with the God light He saw. He could see God in the leper. He could see God in the tax collector. He could see God in the thief at the cross. He could see Himself in everyone.

Consider if we looked in His eyes. The power you would gain in your faith by seeing God in everyone. The knowledge you would gain in recognizing God. The peace you would have that truly passes all understanding.

We always say "The eyes are the windows to the soul." Watch where you look, you may see God looking back at you. Recognize God; don't settle for He is still on the throne. Fellowship and worship with everyone around you. Be like Jesus, meet them where they are. Don't change them, love them.

Who is your gardener? Who is your Mary Magdalene? Who is your Nicodemus?

Golden Gloves

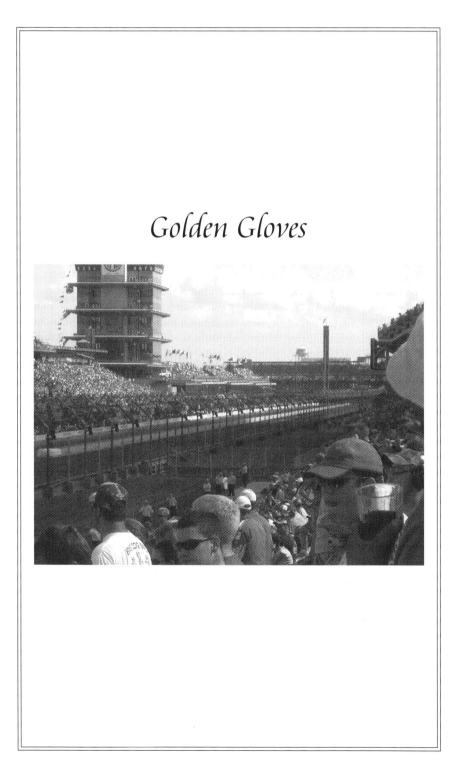

Everyone knows the phrase "Nice guys finish last" but may be not. I have often been accused of having a big heart. Caring more for everyone and animal more than I probably should. I have often accredited my ability to be nice to others as part of my Christian childhood. I remember every Sunday ending junior church with the "Golden Rule."

> So in everything, do to others what you would have them
> do to you, for this sums up the Law and the Prophets.
> Matthew 7:12 (NIV)

We, of course, utilized the King James Version. For every word, we would act as though we were sliding on a pair of gloves. All my life I have striven to be a bright moment in people's lives, always caring and reaching out. Ironically, I usually did all this "kindness" to keep good "karma."

I no longer act kindly only hoping to receive kindness back from others, but to attempt to find heaven on Earth. Imagine if everyone took the hints we are given of needing to help another and we acted.

> Ask and it will be given to you, seek and you will find,
> knock and the door will be opened to you. For everyone
> who asks receives, he who seeks finds, and to him who
> knocks the door will be opened. Which of you, if his son
> asks for bread, will give him a stone? Or if he asks for a
> fish, will give him a snake? If you, then, though you are
> evil, know how to give good gifts to your children, how

much more will your Father in heaven give good gifts to
those who ask him! Matthew 7: 7 – 11 (NIV)

The scripture before the "Golden Rule" is about us asking, why does
He throw the two basically different subjects together? If we ask Him,
seek Him, knock at the doors, we will find Him, and then He tells us to
be kind to one another. He went from talking about us to talking about
others in a blink of an eye. Kind is having a tender and helpful nature
toward another.

I was at the local gas station one day when the cashier was explaining
that the young couple had pumped too much gas. Apparently, the young
lady had purchased some items and the gas, thinking that the cashier
would preset the pump; she could pump the gas when she returned to her
vehicle. Meanwhile, the young man had exited the vehicle and pumped
the determined amount. The girl left the exited the store, and proceeded
to the pumps. Not realizing what had happened while she was in the
store, she pumped over the limit of gas into the vehicle.

Apparently, the gentleman did not think to tell the young lady to
stop pumping, but here they were over their limit in gas. The cashier was
waiting to write down their license for driving off and not paying. I could
see the young lady attempting to make several calls on her cell phone, but
there were no answers. Stress was writing itself all over her face and body.
I could see her searching her vehicle for a miracle stash of cash.

At this time, I was unemployed so having cash in my pocket was rare.
I had gone to the bank for some money for my son's track meet earlier
that afternoon. However, he had gotten sick, so we were not going.

I walked slowly to my truck. I had my hand in my pocket on the cash.
Before I could think, I walked over and gave the money to the young lady.
She was amazed. She tried to explain that she would not be getting any
cash back and I smiled and winked it was okay.

I walked away, got into my truck and drove away. In that moment, I saw Jesus standing there needing gas money and unable to connect with anyone. I could have walked away, it was not my problem. The gentleman with her should have said something. Yet, I did not see this as a point about them, it was about me. If I ask, then I shall receive, that was the point of the Golden Gloves. I can make heaven on Earth by answering to others.

What is funny though is how easy it is to be kind face to face and difficult car to car. I have been a traveling service engineer and have taken many family vacations around this great country. I have found it extremely amazing how much people's personalities change when we are driving.

I had been up all night long on a service call one day. It was early on a Sunday morning as I drove back towards my apartment. I admit I was really tired and irritable from being up all night long, but still.

I was driving down a state highway around 55 miles per hour, when a car pulled out in front of me on a blind curve. Unable to swerve and pass the person in the other lane, I immediately hit my brakes to slow up. The vehicle slid in a fishtail motion, every piece of equipment and tool moved towards the front of the vehicle. I somehow maintained control of the vehicle, barking up the brakes all the way.

The person did not increase his or her speed. As a matter of fact, less than a mile down the road the vehicle turned into a church parking lot. There were no vehicles behind me when this person simply pulled out in front of me, virtually causing a wreck between us. I suppose being kind to one another does not cover our driving.

This was not my first time of having someone, with a Christian symbol or bumper sticker, pull out in front of me. I have traveled many miles and have found being around a church dismissal times on a Sunday is dangerous.

I wander if we forget the Golden Rule as adults or if we just put on racing gloves and not the Golden Gloves when we drive. The scripture says "so in everything you do"; this would mean driving as well.

If we do not want someone to pull out in front of us or our family and cause a wreck, then we should not pull out in front of them. We should be kind, and wait until after they pass before we go. We should want to be the last and not always the first.

We were driving on the way to church one Sunday. We had just reached the downtown area, where exit ramps seem to be every where. A semi was traveling in the right lane, when someone came off the exit ramp and pulled straight into traffic. The person made no attempt to increase in speed. The semi had no time to slow down. He was in the middle of an accident waiting to happen. I needed the middle lane for the split that was coming. I quickly veered into the far left hand lane, giving the semi a lane to exit into. As I passed the semi, the driver was practically hanging out the window saying thank you. I merged back into my lane, and again, he flashed his lights showing his gratitude.

We all know in that moment, he was seeking God's for help for a newly constructed lane, and there I was either to help or to drive pass. I have watched many people with the "WWJD?" bumper stickers stay in the lane. Really, Jesus would cut people off?

Our responsibility as Christians is to be helpful to anyone who asks, seeks, and knocks. So far I have demonstrated that being kind in all things we do, is noticing the person who is asking or seeking.

Now consider a remarkable lesson that took years to learn. My mom had decided that she would be part of the church team that went to the local nursing homes and visited the elderly. She went every week for about a year, and then she approached our family with what was next.

She was going to start bringing one person home for the day with her each week. This meant that once a week, my mom was bringing some elderly person to our house for the day. The person could be a male or a female; she would just see which one was able to come and wanted to come. For over a couple of years my mom would bring home someone new from the nursing home each week. My brother and I would disappear, you know how kids were.

Several years, I mean, several years have passed since those days. We were sitting in church this past week, when the minister told the story of a gentleman with cerebral palsy. The gentleman had lived with his mother until her death, having no family he was forced by the state into a nursing home. The motivation of the story is that it was several years, later when someone was kind enough to hear the gentleman knocking at the door to be in a home: To be in a place where you smell good food cooking.

I was driving home when the thoughts about how my mom's actions of bringing people into our house so many years ago. She must have heard them knocking at the door, wanting to smell the good food cooking, to hear kids running through a home.

The thought then grew in my mind, may be because I have a tendency to challenge even my own thoughts. The point of being kind to one another was to find heaven on Earth. Think about it. If we all took the time to care and be helpful to each other would we really have the towns, states, nations, and world that we have?

It was not costly for me to answer that girl's prayer for money. It was kind of me, and if I was kind to her, if she is kind to someone else later, then ponders on my little investment. If I see the driver seeking a way out of a bad situation and assist, and if later that kindness is returned to someone else, then think of the simple gesture. If we all listen for the knock at the door, and we open the door, then think of the heaven we can make.

If you were lost in a town far from your home, would you not want someone to be kind and give good directions to you? If you had left the gate open to your backyard and your dog went for a stroll, would you not want someone to be kind enough to help you find your dog? If you were camping and a storm hit, would you not want someone to be kind and open the door you stood at knocking?

Being kind to each other is not just opening the door at the store or holding an elevator door. Being kind is trying to make heaven on Earth. It as the commercial states, kindness is an investment that has a large harvest when passed on to others.

Most of us would not stand by and not help a person who had slipped on a cliff and was hanging by a root. We would call for help, we would look for a way to help, or we would knock trees if that would help pull the person back up from danger. This is the charge we have been given by Jesus.

I have my gloves on in order to build heaven, what type of gloves are you wearing? Boxing? Insulated? Carpenter?

You are Related to Whom?

Family reunions are so interesting and funny. I remember a couple of the reunions my parents drove us to in Tennessee when we were younger. The common question was: "Now you are related to whom?" and each time I would have to give my grandfather's name. At the big reunions, even your parents are still asked the question of whose they are.

I was sitting at a dinner one night with some friends when we started talking about another friend who had begun to be really involved in her church. The discussion started centering on how she was happier with her "church family." A couple of my friends had no clue about this phenomenon: church family.

I thought about my time in churches and knew that each time I had another family. Each church family has been different but yet the same. The family is a social unit living together, a group of people descended from a common ancestor. Yet, most church families do not live together; we are descended from a common ancestor. This common ancestor makes our bonds extremely tight. One family pushes towards social goals, the other family pushes towards spiritual goals.

When church family members get together, we don't ask to whom do you belong we know.

> He replied to him, "Who is my mother, and who are
> my brothers?" Pointing to his disciples, he said, "Here
> are my mother and my brothers. For whoever does the

will of my Father in heaven is my brother and sister and
mother." Matthew 12: 48 – 50 (NIV)

We have been taught that we are God's chosen through Abraham,
but it is much more a blessing to hear Jesus say we are His family.

I remember when my son was born and having difficulty during
the delivery. Within minutes of my first conversation to the church,
we had a prayer circle going and people on their way to be present in
prayer; a minister that drove miles to lay hands and pray. The family
was as anxious as us. There is no greater relief than to know you can call
someone and being unable to speak, words are understood and actions
are taken.

I realize that earlier I wrote concerning church and being outside,
and us locking ourselves up away from others and God, but there are also
blessings in the church family. The key is not to limit your church family
to just those in your building.

At our church, every Sunday we go around passing the peace to
each other. We have had ministers standing up in front of the church
wondering if they were ever going to speak. But there is something
peaceful, something spiritual in the hug of fellow Christians.

Sunday may be the beginning of the week on most calendars in the
western world, but it often feels like the end. I have plenty of days been so
tired that I have felt that I could not go on. Then here comes the passing
of the peace.

I played a lot of sports in my youth. I think my parents kept me busy
to use up all my energy and keep me focused on my grades. In one of
my worst moments, I went up for a lay up came down and destroyed my
knee. There I was out on the court in so much pain and needing some
assistance. Then out of no where, I hear my dad explaining that he was
an EMT and my father so he would be attending to me. He hugged me

and carried me off the court. The hug was so engulfing so healing at that moment that I often remember the worst moment as the best.

Those hugs on Sunday are much like that. Work days and family times have ways of draining your spirit from you. Then you walk up to another Christian struggling on the highway, and each of you embraces. The spirit passes through each and yet surrounds each of you. This is true moment of church family. The time when you are hurting beyond words, and they reach out, and say something as simple as "Peace to you."

If we are truly part of Christ, then the real power of restoration comes from knowing that each hug is from God.

> How great is the love the Father has lavished on us, that we should be called children of God! And that is what we are! 1 John 3:1 (NIV)

There are studies that insinuate that twins have an inner connectedness. They can know when the other is hurting, sometimes before the one hurts. This is possible in God as well.

Ever walked into church on Sunday and tried to put on a face that everything was okay? You make it to your seat. You make it through the service, but then on your way out, it happen, someone stops you and asks and you cannot hide the pain. You talk, you pray, you hug, and you feel the love.

A closing thought: Your family is there for when you need them, but they also have an obligation to be there for you. If you call your brother in the middle of the night for a jump on your Blazer, he will come, but he may not be the happiest camper in the woods. Obligation is not part of a church family member's characteristic.

"My prayer is not for them alone. I pray also for those

who will believe in me through their message, that all of them may be one, Father, just as you are in me and I am in you. May they also be in us so that the world may believe that you have sent me." John 17: 20 – 21 (NIV)

Jesus did not pray for just himself and his disciples, He prayed for us long before we arrived here. He called us to be one in Him as the Father is one in Him. He gave us a common ancestor greater than Abraham.

Have you found your family yet? The family consists of people sharing common beliefs and activities. How do you think you can make the journey alone when even our Lord had family?

The Spiritual Phone Network

It was early one morning when the name hit me like a ton of bricks. Bam! I had not thought of her in years. I thought about our last conversation and how time had separated us more than the miles. I smiled and quickly said "Lord, watch over her," then proceeded on with getting ready for my work day.

The day was typical, moving from one task to another. By the time I got back home my thoughts of the morning had escaped me and I forgot to take the time to call my old friend.

As time passed by friends were still not connecting via the phone but thoughts and prayers were exchanged on a periodic bases without much thought.

It was when I was a little country girl that the minister spoke of names moved by the spirit. He preached about how we have names prompted into our thoughts, and our job is to pray for them at that moment. It was God's request for you to get involved in His love.

> In Damascus there was a disciple name Ananias. The Lord called to him in a vision, "Ananias!" "Yes, Lord," he answered. The Lord told him, "Go to the house of Judas on Straight Street and ask for a man from Tarsus named Saul, for he is praying. In a vision he has seen a man named Ananias come and place his hands on him to restore his sight." Acts 9: 10 – 12 (NIV)

Then Ananias went to the house and entered it. Placing his hands on Saul, he said, "Brother Saul, the Lord-Jesus, who appeared to you on the road as you were coming here-has sent me so that you may see again and be filled with the Holy Spirit." Acts 9: 17 (NIV)

Of course, like most kids, I sat there in that little church trying to count down how much longer this preacher was going to be talking. I think it is totally amazing how you hear something; and yet, act not on it at that moment; but later you do act based on that dust bunny in the brain. The Spirit moves between each of us and we are connected to each other to act as the Spirit guides, so when names appear on the heart, it is our responsibility to pray. How does the spiritual network function?

Ever looked at the cross and been told what the symbol of each pole represents? The horizontal bar represents human to human connections; and the vertical bar, represents God to human connections. In other words, due to the cross we can connect to each other's spirits and to the spirit of God.

The spiritual network is the cross; we connect to each other's spirit through one tower. In the moments of friends coming to our minds, one feels the prayers of that person and the Holy Spirit pressing on you to act and pray as well; hence the command, "Pray continually," 1 Thessalonians 5:17 (NIV).

How do we know that we are to work together? How do we know that we are connected together?

Jesus sent the disciples out two by two. He calls people to join the body of Christ; we are not here to have to stand alone. We can reach each other and be thankful. At these moments, you will find that when your friend's names pops into your heart, you do not have to know the need, just the name. You simply ask quickly that God be with them. You are not responsible at that moment to understand their needs you are responsible for the action, the needs will come later, if necessary.

Sitting in church one Sunday, during the lessons from the Contemporary Bible (which is a part of our service where we continue Biblical stories with the people of today's lives), I heard a heart breaking story of how the school had decided that a particular student was not to come back to school because he was unable to learn. Really, a student unable to learn? What if it was the school that was unable to teach?

Of course, the lesson from the New Testament was how Jesus healed the paralytic man. Unfortunately or fortunately for me, I was unable to get passed the first few passages and not into the real lesson by the minister.

> A few days later, when Jesus again entered Capernaum, the people heard that he had come home. So many gathered that there was no room left, not even outside the door, and he preached the word to them. Some men came, bringing to him a paralytic, carried by four of them. Since they could not get him to Jesus because of the crowd, they made an opening in the roof above Jesus and, after digging through it, lowered the mat the paralyzed man was lying on. When Jesus saw their faith, he said to the paralytic, "Son, your sins are forgiven."
> Mark 2: 1 – 5 (NIV)

Like everyone else, I left Sunday and came a few more Sundays after that before finally the gnawing in my stomach could be stood no more. I approached the minister and asked to get connected with that family. I was unemployed at the time, had plenty of free time on my hands, and had been working with students not passing required tests, so would be willing to assist. I assumed I would be an answer to that grandmother's prayers.

Now back to the New Testament lesson for a minute. It was not the faith of the paralytic man that healed him; although, I could suspect that he nagged his friends to death. "Hey come on, Jesus is in town, you have to get me in there, He can help me." However, as it happened, Jesus healed him, "when Jesus saw their faith…." It was because four people took the time to carry him down there. Not satisfied that they could not get inside, they climbed onto a building and cut a whole in the roof, carried him up to the roof, and lowered him down in front of Jesus.

If your friend was paralyzed would you not do the same? The call you receive from the spiritual network is just that. A friend is paralyzed, trapped on a mat, are you going to pick up a corner, carry him or her to God in prayer? Lucky for us, God is every where, so we don't have to carry people down dusty streets to crowded houses. We simply need to stop and lift up the name to the Lord in a prayer.

The child deserted from school system is being lifted up by his grandmother. It was my obligation to contribute. Do I expect a miracle? No, the real miracle had happened, she cried for help and I answered. You can sit on the sidelines looking for miracles like the generation in Jesus time, or you can be like Jesus and be part of the miracle.

Our miracle may be that he sees others willing to care, and he makes appropriate choices from here. The desire to never want to disappoint and he become a successful person. The miracle may be that he graduates, goes to college, becomes a successful professional and helps his grandmother escape the ghetto. Either way, the miracle has already happened. We have connected as a community.

Names come to mind or heart, prayers are lifted up in silence. Connections are made, people walk out in faith for others, and someone is healed.

Ironically, the people of Babel attempted to build a tower up to the heavens to make a name for them, see Genesis chapter 11. However, God made a tower from two pieces of wood. We are all connected through the cross.

If you reach out, then at the same time He reaches down. What a connection!

For many years, I was on the receiving end of this spiritual network. Every year, I volunteered to take the Christmas care package to the family that my corporation had adopted for the season. Each time we went, we would receive praises from the families. The last was the most memorable. I went with an inside salesman who was very cynical of what we were doing. He was under the belief that people are poor from punishment and not doing for themselves. How this view would change!

We took in the packages; both vehicles took us ten trips to unload. Each time we walked in and each time we walked out, the grandmother could be heard in her bedroom praying and thanking God for our delivery. The mother and grandmother prayed with us after we were finished and told us we were blessings from God. I believe that he now volunteers every year and is one who brings in the most each year.

They had prayed, we had answered, and God delivered.

So the next time, you review your phone, cellular, and internet fees remember that you are also connected the most powerful network and it's FREE!

Have a nagging name in your heart or mind? Why have you not prayed? It is our responsibility to lift our friends and family up to God in prayer. We are not here alone, and how else to feel connected than on the Spiritual Network? Your friend is paralyzed on a mat, what are you going to do?

Angels without Wings

A ngels appear quite often in the Bible, ever wandered why no one believes in angels today? I often question how people can believe in the Bible but yet not believe that angels exist today. It seems like they are setting themselves up for a limited God. To think that God was involved on a daily basis in the lives of the people of the Bible; and now to believe He is not is present in ours is bizarre.

I have heard people state that they believe God is really busy in this time of humanity that He is working on the big things and has limited time for each of us. I argue that we have lost our sight of angels and that God is as busy in our daily lives as the people of old.

By definition, angels are to be messengers. In our story telling ways, we have transposed the supernatural to be the only way to consider an angel, but I argue that angels are simply messengers. Therefore, by being messengers, they may be in human form.

> Then Jonathon said to David: "By the Lord, the God of Israel, I will surely sound out my father by this time the day after tomorrow! If he is favorably disposed toward you, will I not send you word and let you know? But if my father is inclined to harm you, may the Lord deal with me, be it ever so severely, if I do not let you know and send you away safely." 1 Samuel 20: 12 – 13 (NIV) Jonathon said to David, "Go in peace, for we have sworn friendship with each other in the name of the Lord, saying, 'The Lord is witness between you and me, and

between your descendants and my descendants forever.'"

Then David left, and Jonathon went back to town. 1
Samuel 20:42 (NIV)

David's messenger for safety from Saul, King of Israel, is Jonathon,
son of the King of Israel. There was no supernatural being from heaven
sent to warn David of Saul's intent to kill him. He had a friend: A good
friend.

Ever have one of those days when everything seemed to go wrong,
or at least not to your liking? The day seemed to be against you from the
start. Your hair was not cooperating, the dogs did not want to go outside
and get placed in their kennel, the kid is dragging his feet all the way to
the Jeep, you get to work only to see so much work you think you are
doomed. Lunch comes and goes without you, the energy in your mind
and body are both drained.

You rush home, make dinner, and finish homework, your zapped
nothing left. You read the bills and see a notice of a mistake on one of
your accounts.

The next day, some how you found a minute to make that phone call,
your stomach stirs and flips, they did not receive that payment, and worse
yet, you spent that money not knowing.

Great, you are now working yourself to death and you have missed a
payment on the vehicle you need to get to work. You don't have extra, don't
you just love that question, what were you planning? I wasn't planning,
okay, I was surviving.

Could another burden hit your back? You look at the calendar, there
is the proverbial straw: Spring Break, a week off WITHOUT pay!

You lay in bed that night trying to find the words to be thankful
during prayer, but for a moment, you are speechless. You drift off to sleep

thinking prayer was more difficult than normal. You think, "Good thing He knows my thoughts."

The next morning you are sitting at your desk when your cell phone rings. You look and a smile creeps over your face, it is your friend from childhood. She says she just thought she would call you and let you know that she misses you. The miles have separated you more as time has passed.

Your day begins to brighten. You head home. You open the mail again dreading what other mistake you had made. There it was a check from another friend from the past. Apparently, he had been compelled to send some of his friend's gifts in the middle of the year to just brighten their days. You look and the gift moves you from a mistake to a bonus.

When your tears well up in your eyes as you look to heaven realizing that you had just met the new angels.

Being an angel can be just as awesome as receiving the angel.

> When Elizabeth heard Mary's greeting, the baby leaped in her womb, and Elizabeth was filled with the Holy Spirit. In a loud voice she exclaimed: "Blessed are you among women, and blessed is the child you will bear! But why am I so favored, that the mother of my Lord should come to me? As soon as the sound of your greeting reached my ears, the baby in my womb leaped for joy. Blessed is she who has believed that what the Lord has said to her will be accomplished!" Luke 1: 39 – 45 (NIV)

Elizabeth was the second messenger to Mary concerning the baby she was carrying. The first was more supernatural and potentially more disbelieving than the voice of a friend.

In addition to the insight that we have angels among us, we get insight the blessing of being an angel.

I had been volunteering in the tutoring program at the church for a couple of years with the same students. One day one of my kids was telling me about the school's planned trip to the Space Center. After talking with her, it became very apparent that she wanted to go but realized that she would not be able to ask her mother or grandmother.

Now, I was in the position that I had no kids of my own at the time. I had an awesome career with a substantial income. I convinced myself that if she went to Space Camp, she might find an interest, and stay in school, go to college, and ...So I went to her mother and grandmother and asked if it would be okay if I paid for the trip. They were very delighted.

The look on her the face the week she was preparing to leave and the stories when she got home made being an angel easy. I felt as Elizabeth must have felt being used by God to help another Christian along our path. Although, I will admit, Elizabeth's message was much cooler.

Consider the times that friends have called out of the blue, think of the times that you have received just enough of something from someone totally unexpectedly, ever consider they be angels without wings? If you stop looking for angels in wings white robes and with heavenly voices, you might find time to be one yourself.

Baa-Baa-Baa Sheep Are We

From basically the beginning of the Bible, God's children and chosen people have been considered sheep.

> Now Moses was tending the flock of Jethro his father-in-law, the priest of Midian, and he led the flock to the far side of the desert and came to Horeb, the mountain of God..."So now, go. I am sending you to Pharaoh to bring my people the Israelites out of Egypt." Exodus 3:1, 10 (NIV)

Sheep are mentioned more than any other animal in the Bible. If you take away the consideration of sacrifices that they are also referred too, then you still realize that God has called us to be sheep. We have needed guidance from the beginning.

Sheep have been domesticated for many years. They flow their shepherds wherever they are led. Sheep are docile, not aggressive animals. Sheep are prey.

Interesting that He chose such an animal to represent us; and how we consider how ourselves. We tend to follow whatever dress trend is in, but call ourselves individuals. If there is a new electronic device out, we have to go check it out for ourselves. Let us not even get started with the twitters and Facebooks. We are followers no matter how much we try to push the image that we are leaders.

Besides the fact that we are followers, we also require companionship. We need to belong, just as sheep need flocks. No sheep survives in the wilderness alone, and neither do people. Prey an animal that is hunted or caught for food, a person who is in the aim of an attack.

God called us sheep because in this cosmic setting, we are prey to all that would take us from the Good Shepherd. I was a young child when I started being told that Jesus was the Good Shepherd. But it was not until I was in my twenties that I felt the fear of being preyed upon.

I was working so many hours being driven to succeed by this statement a professor had told me in college after the job interview. "I see you having great success at that place. Go get 'em" And go get them I was.

Have you ever heard the phrase, "People get promoted to the point that they are not successful"? I was getting there. I had been working in this company for coming up on ten years. I had been successful at everything they had tasked me to do. Then one day, I was moved to the sales team and working on selling software contracts.

I was trained in hardware. I had spent most of my time at this corporation working on a system that was being phased out. Now, I was being promoted to the opportunity to sell software contracts. These software contracts were purchasing future upgrades for a year or two with that particular software version.

Talk about being thrown to the wolves. Now most customers believed, and had validation for their belief, that upgrades were fixes to the programs.

> My people have been lost sheep; their shepherds have led
> them astray and caused them to roam on the mountains.
> They wandered over mountain and hill and forgot their
> own resting place. Jeremiah 50:6 (NIV)

So driven with the concept for success, unable to see the wear down happening to my body and mind, I was brought to an abrupt halt. I was on my way to work one day, when another driver came barreling off the interstate to the stoplight, anticipating me to run the light, he slammed into the rear tires of my Blazer. The accident left me with excessive neck pain, making it virtually impossible to sit for long periods of time.

I was brought out of the wilderness away from the predators, and taken to my resting place. I was rescued from there and brought to a new pasture. I went back to college and sought a degree in psychology to work with kids.

Not meaning to buy her words of encouragement, my professor had led me astray and caused me to roam around a mountain lost. I had heard those words many days, and success was moving up in a company, but roaming me further down a hill. I was lost in a world that I had no where to roam any longer.

Another interesting fact about sheep and the shepherd is the reunion. Shepherds have left flocks to go find wandering strays in order to keep the flock together. The shepherd is ecstatic when he finds the sheep wandering in the wilderness. I know how lost sheep feel, but what is cool is Jesus let us know how the shepherd felt, which tells us how He feels about us.

> What do you think? If a man owns a hundred sheep, and one of them wanders away, will he not leave the ninety-nine on the hills and go to look for the one that wandered off? And if he finds it, I tell you the truth, he is happier about the one sheep than about the ninety-nine that did not wander off. Matthew 18: 12 – 13a (NIV)

When we wander off, He comes looking for us. How awesome is that? Think on it for a minute. You have wandered off away from the flock, just one of so many white, fluffy, baa-ing baa-ing, sheep. He noticed the one missing. I remember the pure joy and elation when I found my two dogs that had gone wandering around our neighborhood.

One day on a side job, I received the dreaded call. The gate had been left open, and the dogs were missing. I rushed home to the neighborhood, driving up and down all the streets. Finally, there they were, just strolling along, checking out the "hood." As I approached in the car, and opened the door, they looked up not surprised and jumped into the backseat. Of course, dogs are predators so they are not surprised or worried, unlike prey.

The joy of being reunited with Jesus after wandering in the wilderness is much more than coming home after being held captive in a far away land. There is the fact that no longer are you as prey stuck, but there is the feeling of rescuing the prey from the predators.

As you wander over the pasture and unsure of where you are and where you are headed, remember that there is one who will always come and find you. To be lost and then found is to be on the verge of death and brought back to life again.

Get Up and Be Alive

There are over twenty references to Jesus healing individuals in the New Testament. There are scriptures of the apostles and disciples healing individuals; and yet, most Christians do not believe the television evangelist who preaches of healings to the congregations. Why?

There are at least three references to Jesus raising the dead, and a couple of references of the apostles and disciples raising the dead. The best anyone would believe today in that similarity would be waking from a long coma, not from the dead. Why?

Why are there so many references to the healing and raising of the dead?

It is my belief that the healings of individuals and raising of the dead still happens every moment of every day.

> While Jesus was having dinner at Matthew's house, many tax collectors and "sinners" came and ate with him and his disciples. When the Pharisees saw this, they asked his disciples, "Why does your teacher eat with tax collectors and 'sinners'?" On hearing this, Jesus said, "It is not the healthy who need a doctor, but the sick. But go and learn what this means: 'I desire mercy, not sacrifice.' For I have not come to call the righteous, but sinners."
> Matthew 9: 10 – 13 (NIV)

Jesus did not come for the righteous but the sinners hint that is us. Have you ever been paralyzed? I was riding around downtown

Cincinnati with a friend of mine to go see the fireworks. We had taken a couple of wrong turns and where we were, we did not know. All of a sudden my friend stated, "Roll them up and lock the doors." She was paralyzed. The city streets were dark, and the neighborhood was not housing any millionaires, but it bothered me that she said this.

Fear keeps us from each other. We fear the new immigrants into our country, state, city, and neighborhood. Instead of looking for a gift in our new neighbors, we build higher fences and buy stronger locks. We pass stronger laws to send them back from whence they came. What are we afraid of?

Afraid that the person who moved into our life may up root some fundamental thinking we have. Think back to the civil rights movement. Many Caucasians did not move from their fears of African Americans until after watching the inhumanities. People may not want to admit it aloud, but many people who could have made a difference earlier were paralyzed in fears.

> Be strong and courageous. Do not be afraid or terrified because of them, for the Lord your God goes with you; he will never leave you nor forsake you. Deuteronomy 31:6 (NIV)

These were the some of the last the words that Moses gave the Israelites and Joshua before he was to pass away and they enter Jordan. You realize there were members among the group who did not want to move forward. You must consider that Joshua was terrified and stuck in fear with having to lead this group.

Moses gave the message of healing to the paralyzed.

Everyone sings "Amazing Grace, how sweet the sound that save a wretch like me. I was once lost but now am found, was blind but now I see."

Do you ever think we may still be blind? We may not be blind to God any longer, but we choose to still be blind to the plight of others.

I remember one day my mom and I pulled into a handicapped parking spot at the local mall. My mom got out of the car, and another driver was staring at her, like take a picture stare. I got out of the car on the passenger side, and mimicked being extremely disabled. The other driver immediately turned her head and pulled away.

I have observed for years how people have watched my mom walk. I have watched people stare to the point that my mom becomes uncomfortable. I guess that day, being a teenager; I had just been moved to a point of touching the untouchable. Before you get mad at me, my mom scolded me and I felt bad, but I did not feel bad for making that driver feel self conscious for staring. The driver was so busy judging my mom's "disability" for that elite parking spot, which she ignored the compassion that should have been in her heart. Yes, there was the infamous Ichthus on the back bumper.

I think in many ways, we as Christians are still blind. We vote in politicians and give to our church and other organizations to help the needy, but we won't go see the needy. We won't invite the person with leprosy to our dinner tables.

> A man with leprosy came to him and begged him on his knees, "If you are willing, you can make me clean." Filled with compassion, Jesus reached out his hand and touched the man. "I am willing," he said. "Be clean!" Immediately the leprosy left him and he was cured. Mark 1: 40 – 42 (NIV)

Jesus touched a man that in those times no one touched. Jesus had compassion on a person, who no others found to be worthy of being considered a human. Think in today's atmosphere, what is our leprosy?

How many people stood by the coffee pots and discussed the fact that HIV was a disease for the homosexuals and drug users? Ronald Reagan had us convinced that it was immoral behavior that caused such a punishment.

When they needed to have compassion and a touch from someone who cared, we were not available. We were concerned with our vulnerabilities and not those suffering.

Now back to the original scripture, Jesus told the Pharisees to go and learn: "I desire mercy, not sacrifice."

Often we are full of pity for those with disabilities or diseases, not compassion. Jesus called us to have mercy, compassion, benevolence, love. Pity should not be part of the word trees for mercy.

I have worked with disabled kids in school and have had one that was my best friend until we moved. As I stated, my mom is disabled, she has cerebral palsy. Thanks to her being my mother, I have learned that pity is a barrier.

Pity limits us from seeing the gifts that everyone has to offer. Pity also puts chains on those who could do more, but we want to take pity on them and help. My mom was told that her education would be limited; she may not perform to standards. For the record, she graduated on the honor roll, before there were "special needs" classes. She would not allow the barriers to be there, good thing my dad had a life line though for Algebra.

Pity by most of us is feeling sorry for someone. I am here to tell you that most of the challenged people I have met don't feel sorry for their position. Therefore, the question is why do we? The happiest kids I met at school each day attended special need classes.

Gone to a funeral lately and seen anyone rise out of the casket? It clearly talks about people being raised from the dead.

> When the Lord saw her, his heart went out to her and he said, "Don't cry." Then he went up and touched the coffin, and those carrying it stood still. He said, "Young man, I say to you, get up!" The dead man sat up and began to talk, and Jesus gave him back to his mother. Luke 7: 13 – 15 (NIV)

Again, His heart went out to the mother from Nain, and He touched the coffin. I cannot count the number of funerals and wakes that I have attended in my life. I realize that there were a couple of people in attendance that were praying for the person to arise. Does this mean it cannot happen? Not exactly.

I venture to say that this was more for those of us who have been serving God from our pews for years. He is calling us to "Get up!" Arise from our traditions and accepted ways. He is calling us to "Get up!" and heal His people.

We have been given permission through the many examples by Jesus and the disciples to find mercy and to get up and rise. We are not to be blind to the oppressed, not be paralyzed in fear of others, scared to touch another. We are to arise from our death of religion and be a follower of a pilgrim. The command has been given: "Get up and be alive!"

Healing begins in us so that through us others may be healed. Mercy and compassion are what lead Jesus to action, not pity. Check you pity at the door, and limit your sacrifices.

Limited Vision

Just graduated high school, life is before you. There are so many choices for you at that time. Do you go to college? Do you go to work? Do you go into the military? Do you travel? There are so many mistakes to be made, at least according to everyone else. Right?

Several years have passed since the day I was standing with the world at my feet. I have gone down this road and down that road, turned here and even made a "U" turn according to some of my friends.

I have had acquaintances judge my route and ask me, "Wander, what you could have done if you had stayed on the right road the whole time."

It has taken all I have to not comment back to them, "Really? You think I am big enough to move outside of God's whole plan." I mean, I have always been taught that God has a plan. He allows free will, but within the free will, He knew our choices and has worked the plan with those choices.

The transfiguration that takes place in Christians after a time is truly amazing. It has been a common theme in Christianity and makes me ask if God cries at our offenses to each other.

> The apostles and the brothers throughout Judea heard that the Gentiles also had received the word of God. So when Peter went up to Jerusalem, the circumcised believers criticized him and said, "You went into the house of uncircumcised men and ate with them." Acts 11: 1 – 3 (NIV)

Acceptance and forgiveness are not the first arms Christians outstretch to others. We judge. How many sermons have we sat through where the message was about "they?" Critical of the beliefs of others, assuming that "one-way" means only our way. In a world of over 6 billion people, we believe our denomination to be the chosen and the way.

The Bible and God, interestingly, have not been so judgmental on people. The Bible does state the laws and does state that God is judge; yet, His actions have been more of forgiveness and less of judgment.

> But the Lord said to Moses and Aaron, "Because you did not trust in me enough to honor as holy in the sight of the Israelites, you will not bring this community into the land I give them." Numbers 20:12 (NIV)

> After six days Jesus took with him Peter, James and John the brother of James, and led them up a high mountain by themselves. There he was transfigured before them. His face shone like the sun, and his clothes became as white as the light. Just then there appeared before them Moses and Elijah, talking with Jesus. Matthew 17: 1 – 3 (NIV)

Moses sinned, was punished, and was forgiven. Many miss the continuation of the story of Moses in the New Testament. Could this be an insight to the true heart of God? A God who punished, forgave, and then blessed. God gave acceptance and forgiveness and displayed another way to the promise land.

Unfortunately, we as a people fail to give such forgiveness or see the other way. We allow ourselves to be separated with the confidence that we are correct. Many of our dividers are based upon variance in interpretation.

Has anyone ever read a book or poem and not receive different insight than someone else? Remember all the English papers we wrote in school, explaining the symbolism we found throughout the book. Remember the teacher always saying there is no right or wrong answers as long as you present a good argument? Then why do we demand only one interpretation of the Bible?

Are you ashamed of the fact that the only scripture you read is on Sunday morning? Many of today's Christians are so busy in their daily lives that they rarely take the time to read the actual Bible. We might read daily devotions, someone else's interpretation of scripture. We allow others to feed us the words of God. We do not seek them ourselves.

Have you ever been out in the woods and dependent upon one set of eyes to get out? Do you walk through a museum and allow only the curator to explain what is in the art work, not looking for yourself?

In the scripture above, when Moses was on Earth as a human, there was no discussion in the Bible concerning eternal life. The way to God had not yet been paved by Christ's sacrifice. The Mount of Transfiguration provides two insights into God's forgiveness and plan.

First, Moses was forgiven. If Moses was not forgiven, why would he be on the Mount in the Promise Land with Jesus and Elijah? God gave him the gift of being in the Promise Land. It was later, but he still arrived to the Promise Land.

Second, Moses was with God and he got there before Christ's sacrifice. Yes, there is one-way to God, and it is through Jesus Christ. However, God's highway does not run on a north-south, east-west directional map. Meeting Jesus where you are; is totally different than meeting Jesus where I am.

Experiments have been performed to demonstrate that people learn differently, especially in our school lessons. If we learn our A, B, C's and 1, 2, 3's differently, then don't we learn our Christianity differently?

Review the way Jesus called His disciples, the way He interacted with the different people.

Have you ever visited a different church while on vacation? Did you feel uninvited? Did you feel like the third wheel on a two wheel bicycle?

Churches should be places where we open our doors to all our brothers and sisters, not where we stand just like the apostles in Acts stood. How can we still see others as unclean, undeserving of God's forgiveness? At least the apostles have the excuse of the faith being new and not understanding all of God, what is ours?

I go back to those who have commented on my journey. If I did not take the path that I had taken, then how would God be able to use me totally? As a child and youth, my life was very sheltered in southern Indiana. I had limited vision of others. I had limited vision of God. My friends have limited vision of God's plan.

A person's natural instinct is to judge that which we do not understand. If I stayed where I was, I would be more judging of others and less empathetic.

> The word of the Lord came to Jonah son of Amittai, "Go to the great city of Nineveh and preach against it, because its wickedness has come up before me." But Jonah ran away from the Lord...Then they took Jonah and threw him overboard, and the raging sea grew calm. At this the men greatly feared the Lord, and they offered a sacrifice to the Lord and made vows to him. But the Lord provided a great fish to swallow Jonah, and Jonah was inside the fish three days and three nights. Jonah 1: 1- 3a 1: 15 – 17 (NIV)

When God saw what they did and how they turned from their evil ways, he had compassion and did not bring upon them the destruction he had threatened. Jonah 3:10 (NIV)

> But Jonah was greatly displeased and became angry.... But God said to Jonah, "Do you have a right to be angry about the vine?" "I do," he said. "I am angry enough to die." But the Lord said, "You have been concerned about this vine, though you did not tend it or make it grow. It sprang up overnight and died overnight. But Nineveh has more than a hundred and twenty thousand people who cannot tell their right hand from their left, and many cattle as well. Should I not be concerned about that great city?" Jonah 4:1, 9 – 11 (NIV)

Jonah flees the request of the Lord thrown overboard by others, swallowed up by a big fish to sit and think about his choices. He prays a prayer to the Lord of praise inside the belly of the big fish. He then goes to Nineveh as originally requested, notices a decree that everyone is turning the evil ways in hope that God will not punish them. Jonah gets mad, goes to the wilderness, sits down, and goes to sleep. God covers him with a vine and the next morning the vine dies. Apparently, this is making Jonah mad enough that he is giving up. The vine is the last straw. But God directs his sight back on Nineveh.

Now, many people know this story, I mean who can forget a person being swallowed up by a big fish? But take a look, the path that Jonah took caused the men on the boat to turn towards God. The storm had brought them into faith and sacrificing to God. Would they have changed their ways if he had not gone that way?

Nineveh, a town where people did not know their right hand from their left; know any of these people? Sure you do. Jonah judges them for their reasons of turning, in his mind, using God's compassion and slow to anger characters to continue on their paths. He did not have compassion, he grew in frustration. How can we serve a God full of compassion and yet, be so judgmental?

In complete vision Jesus forecasts the future:

> For Jonah was three days and three nights in the belly of a huge fish, so the Son of Man will be three days and three nights in the heart of the earth. The men of Nineveh will stand up at the judgment with this generation and condemn it; for they repented at the preaching of Jonah, and now one greater than Jonah is here. Matthew 12: 40 – 41 (NIV)

What a vision. The people of Nineveh, who had made Jonah so mad by their ways, the people of Nineveh, whom God found compassion, will be the judges of the next generations' sins. Can you imagine Jonah's face in heaven when he heard that?

I imagine his jaw dropped, his limited vision never saw that coming. He saw no reason to try to save such a corrupt place, and this place becomes the judgers.

The experience must have been similar to when you read a book and then go to the movie. If no one had told you, you would have not made the connection between the two. At least that has been my experience.

I remember reading Star Wars, all nine books. I had enjoyed every book. It took my imagination to so many places and forms. Good writers point you in the directions, but they leave the whole vision upon the reader. However, when I went to the movies, I was truly disappointed.

The movie gave only a limited vision. I was seeing the characters of some producer, and trust me some of them were not as good as the ones I had envisioned.

So let's get back to all these religions all these divisions between people based on interpretations. Everyone sins, unfortunately, we sin more than we wish to admit it. We each have a sickness that requires daily medical attention. The surgeon has not completed all of his work. To stand in judgment of another piece of work is to actually judge the creator of the work.

> "Teacher," said John, "we saw a man driving out demons in your name and we told him to stop because he was not one of us." "Do not stop him," Jesus said. "No one who does a miracle in my name can in the next moment say anything bad about me, for whoever is not against us is for us. I tell you the truth, anyone who give you a cup of water in my name because you belong to Christ will certainly not lose his reward." Mark 9: 38 – 41 (NIV)

So I go back to the original true question, do you think God cries at our every divide that we create? God provided laws that promoted good community. He split the tabernacle between the tribes to allow equality. He called twelve tribes, He called twelve disciples.

There may be one way but there are various paths to the way. Consider Peter and Paul, two very influential apostles of the new church. Peter, disciple, friend of Christ, forgiven three times for his three denials, fisherman; and Paul, apostle, slayer of Christ's followers, educated by Romans, called via being blinded. Read each of their letters and hear different words with unique tones of emphasis. But yet, both made it to Jesus. Hummmm, wander if that means we have various paths to the one-way?

Before you consider someone else a sinner or agree to the group's consensus that they are sinners, ask yourself, and "Is the work complete?" Are you complete? Is God totally complete with making you who you are to become? I know I am not finished. First clue, you are still here.

> I thank my God every time I remember you. In all my prayers for all of you, I always pray with joy because of your partnership in the gospel from the first day until now, being confident of this, that he who began a good work in you will carry it on to completion until the day of Christ Jesus. Philippians 1: 3 – 6 (NIV)

Don't look for the difference in each other, look for the similarities. Look for path that sheds another light on how God is. If we accepted each other in our own faith on our own path, then would we be closer to accepting heaven?

Imagine a supper with one person from every part of life sitting down to eat. After enjoying the various fruits of each labor, would the conversation just not be too cool. To hear God's voice in a different story would that not grow your faith that He is every where? If He has the whole world in His hand, as we sang when we were young, all the peoples of the world, then how can He not be in all the world religions?

Hey, Jonah, get out of the belly of that big fish. Quit complaining that God has found compassion on them. Go and rejoice with them, repent from your evil ways. Did you toil over that vine? Did you make it grow? Use the compassion God has given you, give the forgiveness and openness that God has welcomed you; the time for judging has not come, see Paul's statement, and realize that none of us have been completed yet.

Courage to fight the Big Fight

It could be that I am a little person, but I have been captivated by David and Goliath since I was a child. I was not drawn to the story so much that David, a little guy, killed Goliath, a giant, but just the shock at how much courage David showed while everyone else from Israel was terrified.

> David said to Saul, "Let no one lose heart on account
> of this Philistine; your servant will go and fight him." 1
> Samuel 17:32 (NIV)

David as a young man, the youngest brother went to fight the giant and not let anyone from Israel lose heart. He talked to Saul as though he was scaring off a wild animal.

My mom now has a large husky and this little poodle mix. The little dog is always attacking the big dog. She bites at him and never backs down. I call it the little dog syndrome. I have noticed this little dog complex in many little dogs. They remind me of David, always full of courage against any opponent. They do not see themselves as small, and neither did David.

So what is the point of David and Goliath? There is the point that David had great faith, we are often taught about his faith, but he also had courage. Courage is the character that enables you to face danger or pain without showing fear.

> David said to the Philistine, "You come against me with

sword and spear and javelin, but I come against you in the name of the Lord Almighty, the God of the armies of Israel, whom you have died. This day the Lord will hand you over to me, and I'll strike you down and cut off your head. Today I will give the carcasses of the Philistine army to the birds of the air and the beasts of the earth, and the whole world will know that there is a God in Israel. All those gathered here will know that if is not by sword or spear that the Lord saves; for the battle is the Lord's, and he will give all of you into our hands." As the Philistine moved closer to attack him, David ran quickly toward the battle line to meet him. Reaching into his bag and taking out a stone, he slung it and struck the Philistine on the forehead. The stone sank into his forehead, and he fell facedown on the ground. 1 Samuel 17: 45 – 49 (NIV)

He not only mocked the Philistine that he was going to die, he explained what would happen to his body after his death. In addition, he ran quickly towards Goliath as Goliath was approaching him: No fear only courage.

We are often placed in positions to display our courage, moments to fight against an injustice. I remember one year being at the local zoo. It was a very hot day and very crowded zoo. We were in line for the train that went around the safari section of the zoo. The line was longer than most of the roller coaster lines at most amusement parks. Our son was about four or five at the time. He was obsessed with trains.

As we were waiting in the line, the train pulled into the depot. I pulled my son up to my shoulders so that he could see the train. There was a little boy in front of us who wanted to see as well. He tried to pull himself up on the woman he was with. He did not succeed and stepped on her foot. She became upset and pulled his arm and shoved him away stating he needed to calm down and stop.

I could have been like most of the other people standing there looking at her in dismay, but I am made of courage. This woman was dressed in all black leather: black blouse, long pants, and high heeled boots. Did I mention that it was July and very HOT?

I was with another friend from church. I asked my friend loudly, "Are we at the baboons cage? We must be viewing the baboons, because they tend to pick stuff off their babies. Oh no we are in line for the trains; guess this lady did not realize that I was a psychology student who is supposed to report any abuse."

Ironically, later in the line, when the young boy spilled her drink, she calmly picked it up and walked it to the trash, not saying anything or doing anything to the kid. I guess some people need a social conscious.

We are called to be show courage not in just the face of civil disputes such as the Civil Rights Movement.

We were out to eat one night at the local mall. We had just pulled into a parking spot and gotten out, when four teens come running behind our car. We heard an older gentleman chasing them and yelling. I asked the kids what was wrong and they said he was chasing them and they needed 911. I looked at the gentleman, who had abandoned his car out on a four lane highway, he, too, asked for me to call 911.

I asked again what was going on. Apparently, the teens had given the gentleman the finger while they were running across the highway in front of him. He stopped his car and proceeded to chase them. He wanted to have them arrested for such an act. I explained to the gentleman that I would be glad to call the police, but he would also be in trouble for leaving his car on a busy highway and chasing kids through a parking lot.

Everyone split up and decided to go their different ways. I did not call the police. The gentleman went back to his car, and the teens ran on into the mall.

In both situations, I could have looked the other way, I could have chosen not to act, but as I said I am made of courage. Each of these times, my son was with me. He asked me if I was scared. To tell you the truth, I did not have time to think of repercussions, I just acted.

David did not consider failure when he ran out onto the battlefield. He actually "trash" talked Goliath before the battle. "Trash" talking is what most competitive people do when they are in the middle of competition. Some "trash' talk to scare the competition while other "trash" talks to inspire them.

I spent many years playing organized sports, not always with the greatest of sportsmanship. I remember many of games in which I was doing a lot of talking, and most of what I was saying was to build my own confidence and my teams. Did my trash talking change the outcome of any games? Who knows, it inspired me and my teammates against the other team.

Now, think back, the Israelite army was pinned down, to scared to move, David's "trash" talking was to inspire the Israelites as well. I am not condoning "trash" talking in sports, I am saying though, David trash talked to inspire himself and the Israelites, and if it upset Goliath along the way, oh well.

Moments of courage arise in our daily lives, what will we do in those moments, act or sit? There is a new show on television that puts people in positions of action, so many walk by while injustices are allowed to happen. You would not want your friends to see you on television, why do you let Jesus see you just observing?

Courage is the ability to tell the church that it is wrong in choosing the minister over his wife in a divorce. Courage is standing for the weak when they cannot stand any longer. Courage is not just rushing into a burning building to save lives, or fighting an enemy many miles away from your home country. Courage is the internal characteristic that makes you move for another person.

I was driving to our other office in Cincinnati from Indianapolis one day, and like usual I was running late. As I was driving down the interstate, I noticed a minivan behind me driving up rather fast and randomly changing lanes. Like most drivers, I watched my rearview mirror intermittently to check when it would be passing me. All of a sudden instead of being on my left to pass, the minivan ran down into a ditch and turned around backwards and slammed into a bunch of trees along the right side of the road.

At this moment, I could have used my car phone to call for help not stopping, I mean I was running late for a meeting and had other things to do. I stopped.

I called 911 from my car phone, exited my vehicle and ran down to see if everyone was okay. The local sheriff showed up with his deputies. I could have left after emergency personnel arrived but then I noticed the injustice.

The police were more concerned with what a bunch of African Americans were doing, the police acted as though they were criminals. There was an elderly gentleman that was disoriented and began to wander into the woods. The police were very aggressive with the family not trying to assist the family.

Now most people would get in their rides and leave, but not me. I explained to the police that the driver must have had a medical problem and we should be helping them.

I realize that in our society now days, the police are very suspicious of others, especially African Americans. However, in this situation, it was a family full of grandparents, a mother and her children. I could not imagine how I would have reacted if the police were more interested in us committing a crime instead of helping us. Courage is often a voice to remind people of their true duties.

The people were finally given medical assistance, and I continued on my path to my office. I was late for the meeting, but after explaining why, most of my co-workers understood. They had come to expect this kind of reaction from me.

As you go through your daily experiences, look for the moments when God has called you to be display courage.

> The teachers of the law and the Pharisees brought in a woman caught in adultery. They made her stand before the group and said to Jesus, "Teacher, this woman was caught in the act of adultery. In the Las Moses commanded us to stone such woman. Now what do you say?" They were using this question as a trap, in order to have a basis for accusing him. But Jesus bent down and started to write on the ground with his finger. When they kept on questioning him, he straightened up and said to them, "If any one of you is without sin, let him be the first to throw a stone at her." John 8: 3 – 7 (NIV)

Many people look to this scripture to tell us not to judge others because we do not know the whole crime. Yet look, in this story, Jesus knew this was a trap. He knew the injustice, the fact it takes two to commit adultery; and yet, only one was being punished. He still spoke the truth of the law by Him challenging the authorities and giving her a chance to live.

Courage is in all of us. We have all been called to act against injustices. Are you ready to lay your life, your reputation, your social standing to stand against injustice? Are you willing to truly be like Jesus and stand?

Can you walk out against your crowd, face the giant, and know you will be victorious?

Not one parent or sibling would stand by and watch a child, brother, or sister get attacked by a bear without acting, why do we stand by why our daughters, sons, brothers, and sisters are persecuted?

The next time you see an injustice answer yourself truthfully when asking, "What would Jesus do?" Quick act before that bear devours your family!

Mirror of Love

One of the quirkiest habits I have is trying to spell words backwards and see if there is another word. For the most part, a majority of our words don't create other words. You would think that after years and years of limited success I would have discontinued this but I find the words that can transpose to be interesting. The word "ton" spells "not"; ironically, you ought NOT to pick up that TON of a burden, it'll be more than you can carry.

The most intriguing word combination to me is "dog" and "God." Did anyone else catch that before me? Don't be scared I am not going to mislead you on this thought, as a matter of fact; you may consider adopting a dog when I am finished; important to notice its dog and not pup.

Cain said to the Lord, "My punishment is more than I can bear. Today you are driving me from the land and I will be hidden from your presence. I will be a restless wanderer on the earth and whoever finds me will kill me."
But the Lord said to him, "Not so; if anyone kills Cain, he will suffer vengeance seven times over." Then the Lord put a mark on Cain so that no one who found him would kill him. So Cain went out from the Lord's presence and lived in the land of Nod, east of Eden. Genesis 4: 13 – 16 (NIV)

In scriptures for the most part dogs are generally considered ill-tempered scavengers which are tolerated but not trusted; certainly not admired and loved. Let us consider where Cain was being placed. He was going to a place without God's presence, a place not to be admired or trusted. Even though God was turning His back on Cain, he was also being protected by a mark. What about a dog? Is there any where that we can go, that the Lord is not?

I was in my twenties and enjoying life as most young urban professionals do. Hanging out with my friends, building my career and assets, and wandering in my own world of Nod, it had been a rough road to get where I was going, and in my opinion I was driving all the way. The trip to Nod began a few years earlier.

Seventeen signing a scholarship to a top school for basketball, planning the future career opportunities after graduation, and one lay-up later, my knee was dislocated with several ligaments torn. The scholarship was gone, my family made to much money for me to get assistance in college funding, no future dreams for a minute. The next plan was military; you know the GI Bill, but not an option for me because of the injured knee, no admittance with recent surgeries.

I had gone to church all my life, it seemed if the church doors were open, and we were there. I was becoming a loss for what to do; I felt like I was being punished by God, every door was closing. So off I went, to the land of Nod, walking my own path, blazing my own trails, "He keeps closing these doors, I will find my own doors."

I found a way to get to a vocational college, which actually landed me an excellent career opportunity. I traveled to many different places and met many different people, all the time not giving a thought to God.

Friends of mine had a dog that they kept outside. She was a beautiful dog. So many colors, reds, oranges, tans, whites, all intertwined, and a muscular body shape, much like a dingo. It was funny how much I and the dog bonded. It got to the point that they knew I was on my way, because the dog would stand up on her dog house looking in the direction I would be driving.

I finally moved to an apartment that allowed pets. I asked my friends, and took the dog home with me. It was great. After a hard day at work, long commute home, the dog would greet me at the door, howling, "I love you." The unconditional love was arriving just in time in my life. I had been a loaner, not really reaching out to anyone really, being my own hermit.

One day on the way to work, I was rear-ended by another commuter. A couple of weeks later, I rolled my blazer onto its side. Talk about a bad month, and someone trying to get your attention. As I hung on my side in my seatbelt, the thought that of what are you going to do now in this position came to my head. I studied the situation, and figured out that I could prop my feet on the gear box, hold onto the steering wheel, and then unfasten the seatbelt, without falling onto the passenger door and rocking the vehicle. The plan worked.

I then steadied myself on the passenger door and reached for the driver's door to open. Problem: I was too short to reach the door and use enough force to open the door. I had to reposition myself on the middle compartment and gear box. I then pushed the door open, with the assistance of the gentleman heading in the opposite direction. I jumped off the truck and slid right down into a puddle of icy cold muddy ditch.

Ironically, the lady I was passing in my big rush to get to work, had asked me if I was okay, and I had told her yes. As I jumped from the Blazer, she stated, "Praise God." I, again, being a quick thinker, thought sarcastically, "Yeah, thank God," which is why I hit the puddle and got totally soaked, note the gentleman did not get wet!

I went to the doctor later that morning for the headache and confirmed no major injuries, just bruising from the seatbelt. My doctor, whom at the time, did not attend a regular church, or even profess any religion, and asked me, "Are you going to church?"

He then stated to me, "You need to start going."

Now during all these terrible times and long commutes, I had my dog. There were so many days that I shoved her away when I got home, but yet, she always came right back full of love to share. Through every migraine, dropped dish or cup, the depression, there was my dog. She never let me get too depressed; she never let me lay in my own self pity. She forced me to love her. She was there to listen to me. She would tilt her head and reply in her own simple way. I could not imagine a friend being any closer. She heard my sorrows and disappointments that I was unwilling to share with any human or even myself.

She greeted me every night with a howl that sound so much like "I love you." It was just the kind of greeting and friendship that I had longed for from others. She was the one that could bring me back and she did. She was truly an inspiration that would get me through the toughest time of my life. As my career faded into the dark because of my new physical limitations, she helped me find something that had been missing in my life. If she had not been there to teach me to love another and myself again, I really doubt I would have found my way back. Talking to the dog, taught me how to pray, again. It was a true gift that she was in my life.

I finally think I knew how to relate to Cain. I may have not murdered my brother, but I had killed off the part of me that everyone had grown to know. I had separated myself from who I once was and lost in the land of Nod, I had my dog teaching me how to interact with God.

A dog is such a unique animal for humans. Dogs have been very adaptable to our request. They are so sensitive to the human needs. When we needed protection from the wilds of nature, dogs have been there to eliminate the threats. When we have needed dogs for policing, they have adapted. Now when we request our dogs be by our side as a friend, they respond with tails wagging and loving eyes: Eager to please.

Interesting how a dog is so much like God. No matter how many times you turn your back on God's plans, no matter how many times you yell in prayer at God for the times you are experiencing, no matter how many times you ignore His love for you, and He is still there for you. Dogs are a mirror gift of God's love to us.

They prepare those of us harden shelled to receive love. Take for instance, how dogs are being utilized in prison programs. People that we as a society have thrown away; people who have lost their freedoms in a place without God; dogs that society have thrown away; dogs who have lost their freedoms in a place without God; both joined together to learn to love and live with someone/something else.

> Cain lay with his wife, and she became pregnant and gave birth to Enoch....When Enoch had lived 65 years, he became the father of Methuselah. And after he became the father of Methuselah, Enoch walked with God 300 years and had other sons and daughters. Altogether, Enoch lived 365 years. Enoch walked with God; then he was no more, because God took him away. Genesis 4: 17 5: 21 – 23 (NIV)

As I have read this story over and over from a child, I have always been drawn to interesting points concerning this story. How does a man who committed the first murder, crime between humans, raise a child, his firstborn to be holy in the eyes of God, especially in the land without God?

As I reviewed my time in the land of Nod, I saw the famous "Footprints in the sand." Cain was sent out to learn to love by the mirror of God's love, a dog. If God turns His back, what does that spell? It may be a stretch for you to believe; but ask yourself, why is society finally relying on placing dogs amongst the criminals? What are we hoping for?

If you look into any dog's eyes you can see the gift of love. According to many people, there is no such things are coincidences: dog can teach you how to accept the love of God, true unconditional love.

God was punishing Cain, sending him out into a world without Him, but yet, God is every where. Cain could not face God. Cain could not accept God's forgiveness or love. Cain was fearful of others killing him, he wanted protection. What better to protect and teach than a dog? He would never be alone and in God's wonderful sense of humor He was with Cain all along. I am not saying dogs are God, but if you take the time to consider it, what other "mark" would be reflective of God? What other mark would teach Cain to teach his oldest to be holy? What other mark spells God?

As you start to dismiss me ask one final question to yourself: Why are dogs the only animals that will lick your tears away? Has God not promises to wipe away all our tears?

Did you hear that?

I remember many services we had as teens where we would come forward to the Alter to pray for guidance for our futures. I remember thinking that I was being called but then I never really knew if it was true. As I tried to follow the path to the college I thought I would need to go to fulfill the "voice" I heard. I found every door to be closed.

As time went by I found another path for a career that was way different from the "voice" I heard. I became to believe that I never heard the voice of God.

One night for devotion we read the passage concerning when Elijah heard God's voice.

> The Lord said, "Go out and stand on the mountain in the presence of the Lord, for the Lord is about to pass by." Then a great and powerful wind tore the mountains apart and shattered the rocks before the Lord, but the Lord was not in the wind. After the wind there was an earthquake, but the Lord was not in the earthquake. After the earthquake came a fire, but the Lord was not in the fire. And after the fire came a gentle whisper. When Elijah heard it, he pulled his cloak over his face and went out and stood at the mouth of the cave. Then a voice said to him, "What are you doing here, Elijah?" 1 Kings 19: 11 – 13 (NIV)

As I lay there thinking about the passage, and my history of experiencing the voice of God, my mind wondered. I lay in a state of dreaming and meditation but very much awake to what I was thinking. In this dream state, I recalled the various trips that I had taken on service calls across the Midwest. I recalled times out of no where I would start marveling at the landscape.

I recalled the times that I would be driving and start whistling old hymnals from my past, unable to recall most of the words, but remembering the melody. I startled myself out of this state realizing that I had been hearing the voice of God more than I could imagine.

It is hard to explain. To explain this process to an unbeliever is to claim insanity. The voice is the part of your mind, your heart, your soul that argues with your conscious self. You feel it from way deep inside; you feel the tug or feel the comfort that surpasses all understanding.

If you had asked me during my travels if I was considering the thought that I was hearing the voice of God, I would have claimed them to be insane. I would have stated that it was just my mind wandering, but it is not the truth. I heard distinct questions. I heard questions that made me ask questions about myself.

The voice of God is not loud, it is not scary. It is calming actually.

I had to take a moment to realize that God had been with me all the time. He was talking to me in little voices, and only when I was willing to listen could I actually hear Him.

Part of the problem with hearing the voice of God is knowing what and how to listen for His voice.

I grew up with the generation that had George Burns depicting God in movies. His voice was always wrong in my mind compared to the God I had been taught. I mean I was taught that God spoke with a great voice.

As soon as Jesus was baptized, he went up out of the

water. At that moment heaven was opened, and he saw the Spirit of God descending like a dove and lighting on him. And a voice from heaven said, "This is my Son, whom I love; with him I am well pleased." Matthew 2: 16 – 17 (NIV)

I suppose it was the fact that essentially every time I have heard the story of Jesus' baptism, a male minister has proclaimed in a very loud voice from the pulpit "This is my Son, whom I love; with him I am well pleased." I began to incorporate those loud voices to God's, so George Burns came up short in the movie.

Yet, when I look back on past impressions, I find myself falling short and expecting too much from God's voice because of those old ministers.

When Jesus was baptized, a dove descended from heaven. Doves have a very low and soft cooing sound. It was not until we moved into this house that I got to experience their calls every morning. One has to really listen to hear it, especially on a busy city street.

I explained earlier about how I changed my career from electronics to working with kids based on a little voice. The little voice kept asking me every Tuesday and Thursday, why are you happiest on these days?

After finally acknowledging the question and realizing there was a real basis for the question. I came to the conclusion that I was happiest because I was working with the kids on those days and not the other days. As I studied the situation, because I do nothing without studying the situation, I recognized the voice again.

Have not heard the voice of God? Are you sure? Did you quiet yourself? He is not in the wind. He is not in the earthquake. He will not be in the fire. He is in the gentle whisper coming from a dove.

Quit trying to hear God shouting from heaven. Quit trying to hear

God in the loud discerning voice of judgment. Accept the quiet whisper and the soft messenger, the dove.

Ask yourself this, if God shouted from heaven, would we know who He was talking to?

Grace the Mystical Word

༄

Grace is a word so hard to explain and understand. How can God not only be forgiving but give us grace? What is grace anyway?

In all my years as a Christian grace has been "amazing" to me. I sing of it, I feel of it, but I have trouble explaining it to my son.

Your child does something wrong. For instance, my son broke a window in anger but on accident one day. As he explained it, he was shooting his ball at the wall, and it reflected at the window. As I heard it, he was angry, throwing his ball at the wall, and it reflected off the window. I have forgiven my son, and explained that by grace he did not have to pay for the window. Good example, right?

In today's youth, there is an expectation that I was going to replace the window as his parent, not him. I in my brilliance realize that if my son cannot comprehend my grace given to him, how will he understand God's? I went looking for how we are to understand God's grace, what examples do we see to assist in explaining it?

> When your days are over and you rest with your fathers, I will raise up your offspring to succeed you, who will come from your own body, and I will establish his kingdom. He is the one who will build a house for my Name, and I will establish the throne of his kingdom forever. 2 Samuel 7: 12 – 13 (NIV)

After David had sinned in a bad way by having an affair and then sending her husband to the front line of a war, this was David's answer to building God's temple. One might have thought that David was being turned down by God but David did not see it this way. He was given a great gift from God: grace.

> What more can David say to you? For you know your servant, O Sovereign Lord. For the sake of your word and according to your will, you have done this great thing and made it know to your servant. How great you are O Sovereign Lord! There is no one like you, and there is no God but you, as he have heard with our own ears. 2 Samuel 8: 20 – 22 (NIV)

Being forgiven by God is not enough, He gives us grace. He makes our wrongs right. God could have had the temple built by Solomon and not let David know of the gift. He moves us from places of evil and darkness to mountains on high. David could have just been forgiven. Grace is beyond forgiveness, it is the gift of not paying for the window.

> You see, at just the right time, when we were still powerless, Christ died for the ungodly. Very rarely will anyone die for a righteous man, though for a good man someone might possible dare to die. But God demonstrates his own love for us in this: While we were still sinners, Christ died for us. Romans 5: 6 – 8 (NIV)

I had a friend who I had loaned some money to in order for her to get passed an economic down turn. We had agreed that she would pay me back so much a month once she got back on her feet.

As time went along, it became very obvious that she was never going to pay the money back. Time has continued to pass, I have never mentioned the repayment to my friend; and I have never questioned why she did not attempt to repay me.

I have often thought about why I never inquired. I guess, in some way, I knew when I was giving her the money originally I would not be getting the money back. By the grace of a friend, I forgave her and continued to be friends, never letting money be a divider.

Grace is more than just forgiving.

> When they had finished eating, Jesus said to Simon Peter, "Simon, son of John, do you truly love me more than these?" "Yes, Lord," he said, "you know that I love you." Jesus said, "Feed my lambs." Again, Jesus said, "Simon, son of John, do you truly love me?" He answered, "Yes, Lord, you know that I love you." Jesus said, "Take care of my sheep." The third time he said to him, "Simon, son of John, do you love me?" Peter was hurt because Jesus asked him the third time, "Do you love me?" He said, "Lord, you know all things; you know that I love you." Jesus said, "Feed my sheep." John 21: 15 – 18 (NIV)

Jesus did not only forgive Peter, He asked him three times. Why three times? In the courtyard, Peter denied Jesus three times. Jesus could have just asked Peter one time, but He asked him three times. Grace is going beyond the forgiveness and moving a person to a better place.

Grace is telling your mom you trust her given her "mistakes" with you. My parents were sometimes strict when it came to certain things. My mom could sometimes make me believe that she was here to intentionally to take away my smiles.

I was a typical teenager, no doubt about that, and some of our issues were "normal." My mom had called me home from homes of my friends because she wanted me to be home. She has even driven miles and hours away to come and pull me away from a Christian Youth Retreat. I was having fun when it was not permissible.

Forgiveness to my mom would be to let go of the old pain and not hold a grudge against her. Grace, though, is giving her a second chance. After my son was born and during those early development years, my mom was the person I believed who would watch him the best. As a matter of fact, she was probably one of the only people I trusted to be with him.

To demonstrate forgiveness, one has to move from just letting someone hold your child, and have them feeding and tending your child. I could have just forgiven my mom, I could have just let her visit her grandchild once in awhile. I knew she had changed. I also realized by now being a parent that people do not come with guide books, no easy instruction manuals.

Grace is forgiving a person, allowing a person back into your arms and realizing that the person may never actually say the words, "I am sorry." As you give grace to others, remember God gives you grace.

The other in sight to Peter's forgiveness is for those of us who have known God and have turned away.

I was in my late teens and early twenties. I had chosen my own path to blaze. I thought that I could do more on my own that without God. As I have stated, I was raised in a church, if the doors were open, we went. But yet, I thought I needed to spread my wings and fly, not concerned with the wind.

There were times that people would tell me that God was being good to me, and I would deny it. I would state and believe that I had obtained it all on my own.

When the time came for me to acknowledge my weakness and for me to turn back to God, I found grace. He forgave me much as I imagined

Peter must have felt. After the third testimony to some of my "other" friends, I realized what had happened.

Grace is mystical, because until you can give to another person, you cannot imagine God's grace to you. Unlike love which is easy to learn to accept and understand, grace is unfathomable until you give grace.

> In everything I did, I showed you that by this kind of hard work we must help the weak, remembering the words the Lord Jesus himself said: "It is more blessed to give than to receive." Acts 20:35 (NIV)

Grace is especially awesome and amazing to receive from God than it is to give, how outrageous is that?

Knead Me and then Watch Me Crumble

Are you unleavened, wheat, or white? Or are you pumpernickel? Jesus was the bread of life; we are called to be bread to the world.

Back in the early civilizations bread was an essential part of people's diet, so Jesus referring to us as His bread means that we are to feed the world Him. But what if it was more?

> Jesus said to them, "I tell you the truth, it is not Moses who has given you the bread from heaven, but it is my Father who gives you the true bread from heaven. For the bread of God is he who comes down from heaven and gives life to the world." John 6: 32 – 33 (NIV)

Jesus claimed in various scripture that He was bread. I agree that He feeds us and others all the time. He was the living word, the bread of life for all us.

The process of making bread is very interesting in relationship to us and our roles. Bread is combined, wetted slightly with a sponge or spray bottle, flour added, and then you knead the mix, you sit it aside, allow it to rise for several minutes before you bake it, and enjoy it.

In the realm of what He was saying was: Time to knead. Unlike eggs that you beat or a cake that you mix with a spoon or mixer, God mixes us to His liking via kneading: A hands on process. God gets personal with our molding. Some bread of course takes on a shorter kneading and others a long one, but that is what makes each of unique. Consider how many types of breads are in the world? He is not making the same bread in each of us; we are all to be of different "flavors".

But let's go beyond the fact that we are to be different breads, the process of making, and to what He has given as a real example concerning bread of life.

And he took bread, gave thanks and broke it, and gave it to them, saying, "This is my body given for you; do this in remembrance of me." Luke 22: 19 (NIV)

Most of us recognize this scripture because we hear it every time we take communion. I was raised in a church where we used crackers/wafers for our communion bread. I realize now after being in a church that uses various types of breads what a disadvantage I had.

First of all, by having all these various types of breads, I have experienced new tastes. Giving insight to the fact that we are not just to feed the world but be accepting of the various other types of breads in the world.

The second symbol is the fact that His body was broken before the crucifixion. One Sunday my son and I were communion servers with a group of other members. After we were finished the floor was covered with bread crumbs. Apparently, some members were upset about the mess of crumbs all over the floor. One of the other servers stated, "Symbolic of the Jesus' body being broken."

Looking down at the floor, I could not contain the tears. I am a very good visual learner, probably why I succeeded more in college than high school, more presentations in college. But to look and see millions of crumbs on the red carpet was VISUAL beyond any communion before.

Then he released Barabbas to them. But he had Jesus
flogged, and handed him over to be crucified. Matthew
27:26 (NIV)

Jesus was beaten before the crucifixion as a testimony of the process
we will also go through. We may not literally be flogged as He and the
other disciples were, but we will be whipped in the spiritual world.

It had been several weeks of unemployment with no real calls for
a potential career. I was beginning to feel like I was unemployable
that I must have some type of a disease. The news kept saying that
unemployment rates were dropping and businesses were hiring with an
employment growth over that time. I kept getting emails from various
career engines that average unemployment time is six months.

It was after I had driven up to Indianapolis when the student I was
tutoring text me to say that he would not be making it today. There went
a few gallons of gas into the air for no reason. The wind just added to the
excitement of the trip. I turned around and headed home.

I decided that well there is the afternoon and finally a day that is not
pouring in rain. I could cut the jungle I was calling a yard. I ran around
the yard with the weed-eater and retrieved all the dog toys and large
sticks from the yard. I pulled the mower out of the garage and into the
yard. I had just gotten my mower back from the repair shop a couple of
weeks earlier. I pulled the mower's cord; it started on the first attempt. I
ran one pass across the front section, and then a sound of a jack-hammer
comes from my mower.

I shut off the mower; raise it ever so slightly to see if there is something
stuck in the blade. Nope. I check the turning radius of the blade, appears
to be smooth. I check fluids and looked for some leaks around the engine;
again, it appeared to be fine. I restart the mower.

It takes several pulls, but the mower finally starts, sounds fine, move one step and "KRKRKKRKRKRKR ZING KRKRKRKRKR ZING," louder than fireworks. Out of work, no money, grass growing like wild prairie grass. Weeds higher than the shrub brushes that accent the yard. By the way, after about an hour, the storm clouds began to assemble and the rains began to pour.

Typically, one would not feel so frustrated, but after a several weeks of rejection, after several weeks of unanswered prayers, after wasting gas that I did not have to replace, after trying to make the yard look somewhat presentable, I had hit the wall. I crumbled!

I did not scream out in rage. I did not cry in tears of despair. I crumbled like a piece of the bread on that Communion Sunday. I moved to a new spiritual level. We get to be kneaded and then we must be crumbled to be totally share the bread of life.

Ever wandered why when all things are going bad, they continue to fall upon your shoulders? You rely on the scripture that He will never give you more than you can handle. But if you accept the fact that we must be crumbled, it helps you see there is growth in the struggles of life.

Consider the following assumption concerning relationships: We all bring our own baggage into it. Every friendship and every relationship is brought with past baggage. As we grow with our friends or love one, we begin to loose some of the baggage. In this same concept, we have baggage on our lives that must be crumbled off before we are ready to move into heaven.

> Aware of their discussion, Jesus asked, "You of little faith, why are you talking among yourselves about having no bread? Do you still not understand? Don't you remember the five loaves for the five thousand, and how many basketfuls you gathered? Or the seven loaves for the

four thousand, and how many basketfuls you gathered?
How is it you don't understand that I was not talking to
you about bread? But be on your guard against the yeast
of the Pharisees and Sadducees." Then they understood
that he was not telling them to guard against the yeast
used in bread, but against the teaching of the Pharisees
and Sadducees. Matthew 16: 8 – 12 (NIV)

I was lucky. I went to a small school corporation in the time when
we were still allowing prayer to be in the schools. I have spent several
years working in the same school system in this timeframe and really
understand what is meant by this scripture.

We send our kids to the public school system, being taught by the
Pharisees and Sadducees. Most of us cannot help it, we don't have the
money for private schools, and some of our denominations are closed to
others.

The public school system has been designed for many years on
the basis of science: Explaining things such as creation and geological
features. I am not here to argue the scientific explanations, but I am here
to ask are you teaching anything to your child?

Many Christians today have the habit of not having a Bible and only
hearing the scripture on Sundays. Some go a little further by listening to
Christian Contemporary radio, but for the most part we read our novels,
magazines, and newspapers but not the Word.

I think back to my grandmother. I remember her reading the Bible
every day. She had probably read the scripture through a hundred times
or more in her life: A privilege of being born before the age of television.
One day I asked her why she read the Bible so much, had she not gotten
everything out of it.

Her response was flabbergasting. No.

She was using her scripture time to crumble. Every time she read a verse known to her, she learned something new. A piece of her old baggage was broken. Later in her adult life, she became basically blind and unable to read the scripture. She bought tapes to listen to the Bible being read, again having crumbs fall to the floor.

So back to my day of frustration, as the rain fell and the storm rolled in, I found myself without electricity and a little daylight. A piece crumbled as I read the scripture that has been read to so many of us.

> Blessed are those who are persecuted because of righteousness, for theirs is the kingdom of heaven. Matthew 5:10 (NIV)

Persecution today may not be in the form of torture and crucifixion. Persecution does not need to be physical to do the crumbling. As you are attacked from inside and out, as you grow in strength, you should take the time to notice the crumbs.

The next time you grab the toaster and all those crumbs fall on the counter, take a moment to remember the broken body of Christ, take a moment to examine the baggage that still needs to crumble.

In the scripture it states that we are to remember Him every time we break bread. I realize that some of us have limited this passage to just our communion, but I venture to believe that it was for every time we break bread. We should remember that His body was broken so we will not be alarmed as ours is being broken.

Don't worry with the crumbs; they will be swept up by the wind when it blows. If you are willing to allow some of your friends to break some of your crumbs off, why are you scared to allow Jesus? The next time frustration rears its ugly head, the next time it takes two hours to get home; instead of reading the paper, try the scripture. How are you to know His plan just for you if you allow someone else to tell you? If a friend wrote you a letter, would you have another friend read it to you? Then why is the minister the only one reading God's letter He sent to you?

Laughter and Sarcasm a Gift

Have you ever laughed so hard you cried? Thought you were going to loose all control of yourself? That laughter is a gift from God.

Ever been with that person that would say just about anything? Ask someone a question and regretted it half way through the sarcasm? That sarcasm is a gift from God.

Do you really believe God is stoic? Many people I have met think that God is always serious, but if He is always serious and we are created in His image, why then do we enjoy laughter so much?

> And God said, "Let the water teem with living creatures, and let birds fly above the earth across the expanse of the sky." So God created the great creatures of the sea and every living and moving thing with which the water teems, according to their kinds, and every winged bird according to its kind. And God saw that it was good. God blessed them and said, "Be fruitful and increase in number and fill the water in the seas, and let the birds increase on the earth." And there was evening, and there was morning – the fifth day. Genesis 1: 20 – 23 (NIV)

God made all the creatures in the sea and birds that fly. I have spent many days on Animal Planet and Discovery watching natural videos. Some of the fish and there behaviors are funny. There are fish in the deep cold waters, that a majority of us humans have never seen, except thanks to video and only God sees, which are absolutely something only the creator would appreciate.

Behaviors are even wilder. The creatures of the water have cycles that illustrate the life-cycle on earth. It is so simple to follow, God laughs as we run circles around looking at the complexness of life.

Frog tadpoles are breakfast, lunch, and dinner for bass fish and others every day. If the tadpole escapes the fish traps, it becomes a frog that pursues fish eggs and babies for breakfast, lunch, and dinner. The hunted becomes the hunter and then it begins again.

> When the Pharisees saw this, they asked his disciples, "Why does your teacher eat with tax collectors and 'sinners'?" On hearing this, Jesus said, "It is not the healthy who need a doctor, but the sick." Matthew 9: 11 – 12 (NIV)

Jesus could have just answered the question with His ending response that He was here to call the sinners and not the righteous, but He gave a bigger sarcastic answer.

Ever been asked that rhetorical question that you were not really allowed to answer? Jesus scoffed at them. He answered their question by telling them to "learn what I mean".

In college, I used to irritate my classmates and professors. I basically had a sarcastic answer for every question. Probably went overboard a few times, but to me laughter is a gift you should share with everyone.

It takes fewer muscles for us to make a smile; and yet, we spend most of our time with a look of business. My grandmother told me when I was young, "You can only give someone a smile for free."

For the longest time, I went through life attempting to give people a smile. It is really like a yawn. Once someone smiles or winks at you, you can't help but smile back and feel good for that second.

I have always been sarcastic, attempting to be the class clown. I really enjoying making people laugh. In crowds, you find me in the center cracking jokes and saying responses that everyone else wanted to say. My sarcasm has gotten me into much trouble throughout my life, but I always come back to the fact that God loves to laugh.

> But Jesus knew their hypocrisy. ""Why are you trying to trap me?" he asked. "Bring me a denarius and let me look at it." They brought the coin, and he asked them, "Whose portrait is this? And whose inscription?" "Caesar's," they replied. Then Jesus said to them, "Give to Caesar what is Caesar's and to God what is God's." Mark 12: 10b – 17a (NIV)

All throughout the New Testament Jesus answers questions with sarcasm. Being the proud parent of a fellow basketball "wanna be," every move he makes brings me a smile. I cannot help but think that with every one of these responses God did laughed.

Think about the last time you laughed until you started to cry. Where did the laughter come from? Laughter is the best medicine for pain, and God surrounds us with good medicine both inside and out. Take that deep laughter and enjoy it, you are laughing with God. The next time you hear a sarcastic answer, consider what answer Jesus would have given.

Work through kneeling

I heard of the story of Adam and Eve so very long ago that it often escapes me that the career Adam was called to. Humans we first called to be gardeners.

> The Lord God took the man and put him in the Garden of Eden to work it and take care of it. Genesis 2:15 (NIV)

I remember so many days of my youth working the garden at my grandparents. The weeds were abundant. I spent so many days on my knees pulling the weeds out, trying not to disturb the plants' root systems. I swore to myself never to plant a garden of my own.

Has anyone out there ever tended to green beans? That is a plant that keeps giving and giving, funny how God never utilized it in any stories. I began to hate the month of July. We would go out into the garden and pick all the beans off plants for harvest. At our house, we didn't pull the plants then, because in a couple of weeks there would be more beans for the picking.

I was your typical grandchild who could think of a thousand different things to do besides pick beans. It still amazes me today of how my grandfather always found so many more beans in my row. I know that I checked, because believe me, he was not tickled pink when he found so many "skipped" beans. Each time I would have to crawl back through the row and recheck for beans.

Gardeners spend a lot of their time on their knees. You may spend the first few days riding tractors, walking behind tillers, but sooner or later you will be back on your knees.

Given that every story in the Bible has a point to it, every verse a meaning. The question arises what is the purpose of being a gardener?

Adam could have been called to be a hunter. He had control over all the beasts and birds of the air.

> Now the Lord God had formed out of the ground all the beasts of the field and all the birds of the air. He brought them to the man to see what he would name them; and whatever the man called each living creature, that was its name. So the man gave names to all the livestock, the birds of the air and all the beasts of the field. Genesis 2: 19 – 20 (NIV)

He was given the authority to name the beasts and the birds, why was he given the career of gardener? Yes, I agree humans need more vegetables than meat, but there is a reason we were called to be gardeners.

Fast forward a few generations and a few hundred years, we find the career of Jesus.

> Isn't this the carpenter? Isn't this Mary's son and the brother of James, Joseph, Judas and Simon? Mark 6:3 (NIV)

I have spent plenty of years on construction sites noticing that carpenters too spend a lot of their time on their knees.

Interesting how the two careers pointed to in the beginning of each Testament has to do with kneeling. Catching a theme here?

I believe we were called to kneel. Kneeling is a very remarkable posture. Many times, we consider kneeling to be a sign of submission. People kneel and beg for their lives in the time of drama. However, it is my contention that we are strongest on our knees.

As I said I spent many days in the month of July walking on my knees, and I have spent many hours walking on my knees around construction sites, at the end of the day, your upper body is tired and your legs worn out. The physical strain your body goes through using only part of your strength.

Being that I have been a Christian for many years and not a Christian for many years, I have often been struck by when Jesus was the most powerful. I think of the miracles, the cross, the tomb, and the ascension, but to me His most powerful hour was at Gethsemane.

> He withdrew about a stone's throw beyond them, knelt down and prayed, "Father, if you are willing, take this cup from me; yet not my will, but yours be done." An angel from heaven appeared to him and strengthened him. And being in anguish, he prayed more earnestly, and his sweat was like drops of blood falling to the ground. Luke 22: 41 – 44 (NIV)

Do not misunderstand me. I believe that Jesus was a very strong man. Many of historians and religious zealots have illustrated the strength He must have had to carry the cross after being beaten. He was extremely strong to go back home and be turned away from His own kin. I could not imagine such a thing, since even at the church from my youth; I am still greeted with a hug and warmth.

Looking at the scripture though you see it, an angel came to Him and strengthened Him. After being with the angel, His prayers were so intense that the sweat was like blood.

Have you ever prayed so deeply that sweat poured from your body? Those are the prayers that get God's attention. The prayers come from deep inside with the willingness to let God into your most sorrowful place. The anguish prayer of Jesus was held in a garden.

What was the anguish representing? Many have excused it to being the obstacles that He was about to face: the time before Pilot, the beating, the mocking, the crucifixion, and the dark tomb. But what if it was more?

I believe the anguish was for us. He was not concerned with what was to come for Him. He was concerned for what was to come for His disciples, for us.

> When he rose from prayer and went back to the disciples, he found them asleep, exhausted from sorrow. "Why are you sleeping?" he asked them. "Get up and pray so that you will not fall into temptation." Luke 22: 45 – 46 (NIV)

He went back to His disciples and commanded them to pray. If the prayer that He was praying was just for Him, then why did He command the disciples to pray for themselves, wouldn't He of asked them to pray for Him? If you read the version in Matthew, He went to the disciples twice to command them to wake up and pray.

Jesus before His arrest and trail went to a garden. Jesus, the King and Savior of the Earth, was a carpenter. Man's first career was a gardener. At every beginning, God has summoned us to a simple career of kneeling. Kneeling builds us up to be strong through the power of prayer.

Ironically, while being on your knees pulling weeds or trimming out a room, you can pray and no one knows. You can talk to God in your heart and in your mind, and no one is the wiser.

But when you pray, go into your room, close the door and pray to your Father, who is unseen. Then your Father, who sees what is done in secret, will reward you. Matthew 6:6 (NIV)

The next time you find yourself working on your knees, instead of dreading the future back ache, pray. God has you kneeling for a reason on this day; use it to your advantage.

Disillusioned? Welcome to Prison

Congratulations you have picked up your cross and are following Jesus. Life will be so much easier for you because of God. You have placed all your burdens down, announced your sin before God, the slate has been wiped clean; and now, you are ready to face the world.

Sound familiar? Accepting God into your life is the easy part, now the road of struggle really begins. Life with Christ is not the yellow brick road. As Christians, we do not get a pass from the world.

> When the owners of the slave girl realized that their hope of making money was gone, they seized Paul and Silas and dragged them into the market place to face the authorities. They brought them before the magistrates and said, "These men are Jews, and are throwing our city into an uproar by advocating customs unlawful for us Romans to accept or practice."
>
> The crowd joined in the attack against Paul and Silas, and the magistrates ordered them to be stripped and beaten. After they had been severely flogged, they were thrown into prison, and the jailer was commanded to guard them carefully. Upon receiving such orders, he put them in the inner cell and fastened their feet in the stocks. Acts 16: 19 – 24 (NIV)

Saul was sent to go about communities arresting, beating, and jailing, not living a life of goodness. After Paul had seen the light from God and transformed into an apostle, he was arrested, beaten and thrown into jail himself. From a life of sin, where it appears one is on top of the world, to a life of glorifying God, Paul was not on the yellow brick road.

In my youth, high school was my prison. Everyday was a struggle to stay faithful to Jesus. Everyday, I was pressured and tempted. There were issues of being mean to other students. There were situations that put me in the middle of telling on others or ignoring their wrongs. There were times of loneliness. Being a Christian in the public school system is a test like none other.

Your desire in high school is to survive: To make friends and move throughout the years with limited stresses. Every step in the hallway was a challenge. Let us not even talk about dating, living by the code of no sex before marriage, does not work in that world.

When I asked my youth minister for assistance and guidance, the answer was "Pray about it." As a youth in the middle of a battle, this was no solution. Teens want action not talk, and pray appeared to be talk.

I struggled with the image that had been preached to me from the pulpit: Living with Christ brings JOY into your life. I was not experiencing any joy at high school. The picture of walking in a garden with Jesus was not working for me.

Having such an image stuck in your head can make it difficult to stay the course. I think of other people I have watched struggle with their walk and began to notice a pattern to the walk of faith. It was not an easy road at all to follow.

> Then he said to his disciples, "The harvest is plentiful but
> the workers are few." Matthew 9:37 (NIV)

I have always been intrigued by this verse. I usually apply it in a sarcastic format to some ridiculous task at work that I have been burdened alone with. But if you stop to think, there are many of us who have attempted to harvest the field but fail by the end of summer.

I have also always been instructed that the harvest was the lost, but ask yourself, if the harvest was Heaven does the verse change?

Heaven is plentiful by most accounts through Jesus and the apostles in the Bible. If Heaven is the harvest, then understanding that the workers are few means realizing that working the field is difficult, frustrating and disappointing, causing many to quit.

Growing up in a corn state means plenty of summers one gets to de-tassel corn. Every summer morning you will see the high school kids lined up at the various bus stops to go do their work. There they are dressed in long pants, long sleeves, and gloves in the middle of July. Corn had the exceptional ability to cut you as you cut the tassel. Each week you notice the workers are getting fewer and fewer.

I am not saying that the entire walk with Christ is a prison or labor intensive. I am saying that we have to come to the realization that there are more stories depicting a life of strife and eternal joy later.

So many young Christians begin their walk of faith with the illusion that life is easier with Christ. When temptations arise and problems shake their foundations, they are left defenseless against the evils of life. We spend so much time teaching young Christians the joy and love of God that we don't prepare them for the rough isolating road ahead. We send our young prey into the world with the predators waiting to devour them.

We would not send our child into the wilderness on their own hike, but we do our new Christians. If you watch the attendance of our weekly Sunday services, we notice every Sunday a few less. We tend to fail in our leadership to follow up on what has happened. We allow weeks to go by before someone notices that so and so has been missing.

> Yet it was good of you to share in my troubles. Moreover, as you Philippians know, in the early days of your acquaintance with the gospel, when I set out from Macedonia, not one church shared with me in the matter of giving and receiving, except you only; for even when I was in Thessalonica, you sent me aid again and again when I was in need. Not that I am looking for a gift, but I am looking for what may be credited to your account. I have received full payment and even more, I am amply supplied, now that I have received from Epaphroditus the gifts you sent. They are a fragrant offering, an acceptable sacrifice, pleasing to God. And my God will meet all your needs according to his glorious riches in Christ Jesus. Philippians 4: 14 – 19 (NIV)

While Paul was traveling, while Paul was in prison, the church of Philippians made it their business to be involved with sending him gifts. He was not alone. We always hear about how we are our brother's keeper. Unfortunately, we monitor our brother's behavior and not his necessities.

Ever wandered why Jesus was often referred to as a teacher? We stand as leaders of the Christian faith just that: Teachers. We assume that He was here teaching us the way to Heaven, which in part is true. He was also our example. He was demonstrating our role as teachers.

For our new Christians and ourselves we need to realize that the road is a long journey with much more mountains to climb, dark valleys to walk through and potential time in various prisons. We need to be our brother and sister's keeper, but not by monitoring their behaviors, but anticipating his or her needs.

We need to be disillusioned and accept our term in prison. There is no yellow brick road, God is not our wizard of Oz and is that not the most comforting thought?

Time for Me?

I t took six days for God to create the Earth. Without getting into a scientific or historical argument, let us just agree on the impression we have been given. Six days of work is all God needed, do you get the point that I am getting to?

By definition our week has been defined. We are to work on six of the seven days we have been given. Do you think God came up with the phrase, "All work and no play makes Jack a dull boy"?

> By the seventh day God had finished the work he had been doing; so on the seventh day he rested from all his work. And God blessed the seventh day and made it holy, because on it he rested from all the work of creating that he had done. Genesis 2: 2 – 3 (NIV)

Holy can be defined as spiritually whole or sound of unimpaired innocence, pure in heart, acceptable to God. Have you ever struggled with the fact that on the day we have set aside to be holy, we ask our ministers, choirs and others to work in the church?

Does anyone really know what day the Sabbath is? Some religions utilize Saturday and others Sunday. We devise a calendar to reflect Sunday as the beginning of the week, and yet we celebrate it as the end of the week, Monday being the dreaded beginning.

I am a work-a-holic, which at one time if you asked me, I would have told you it was better to be addicted to work than something else but this is not true or healthy. At least alcoholics have a twelve-step program, there is no program for work-a-holics, as a matter of fact, and that characteristic is adored by the business world.

Ever been in one of those positions when you think if you don't accomplish the task it won't get finished; and well, who knows what will happen then?

As a child you are instructed to find a career that makes you happy. For the most part, we are raised to work hard at everything we do. We begin our inoculation to ourselves in school. We are taught to work hard for success. Strive for success in everything you do, but we forget to teach ourselves and kids how to rest.

Resting is considered to be a state of inaction or freedom from activity. In our new society of twenty-four hour services, we see rest as a weakness. How can rest be a weakness if God commanded us to utilize it?

> Remember the Sabbath day by keeping it holy. Six days you shall labor and do all your work, but the seventh day is a Sabbath to the Lord you God. On it you shall not do any work, neither you, nor your son or daughter, nor your manservant or maidservant, nor your animals, nor the alien within your gates. For in six days the Lord made the heavens and earth, the sea, and all that is in them, but he rested on the seventh day. Therefore, the Lord blessed the Sabbath day and made it holy. Exodus 20: 8 -11 (NIV)

On the seventh day, God rested, was He weak? In scripture, there is not a specific day given to the Sabbath, it states on six days you work and on the seventh you rest.

As a computer field service engineer, I often found myself working past twelve hours and all seven days of the week. There were times that I thought I had worked the whole year away without much consideration.

After several years, I found myself extremely exhausted and uninspired to go to work. I began to become irritable at the slightest things. I had come to the end of the smorgasbord and found myself unable to refill my plate.

I changed careers and began working in the school corporation. After a time, it was obvious that I was spending more time at school than in my own house. When one makes the constant mistake of calling work home, then one has a problem.

It was at this point that the boiler had reached a boiling point, and the tea kettle sounded. It was my son who gave me the insight as to what had happened as I left the school for the last time.

"God is giving you a rest," that was his statement concerning my unemployment. I had spent so much time working that I had neglected to take time to rest.

In our rush to perform all our duties, we often neglect the crucial point of our life called rest. Work-a-holics are usually sleep deprived.

Sleep deprivation has been attributed to such diseases as diabetes, heart disease, psychosis and bipolar disorder. Without a good night's sleep and rest, we make more mistakes; we have issues communicating and increased stress levels.

Let us put aside the fact that God has communicated to so many of the prophets and kings in dreams and review the state of dreaming. Dreaming unifies the body, mind, and spirit. It provides you with insight into your own self and a chance for self-exploration. Have you ever went to bed with a problem on your mind and awoke in the morning with the solution?

The Sabbath may not be an official day on the calendar for some of us, depending on our schedules, but we must find time to rest. Our God was so concerned with our whole being that He commanded it.

Holy is to be spiritually whole, and rest is the state of freedom from activity. Remember when you were really sick? The doctor or your mom told you to get plenty of rest. What?

Rest is the state of freedom from activity, but yet, our bodies heal themselves while in this state. I wander....

In rest, on the Sabbath, our souls have the ability to recuperate. God called us to rest in order to repair our wholeness. Awesome, only with God can repairs happen in our life while we are totally still.

> "Be still, and know that I am God; I will be exalted among the nations, I will be exalted in the earth." Psalm 46:10 (NIV)

Little scriptures throughout the Bible give us clues about this wonderful healing power; it is up to us to take the time.

Before you schedule that next task, find your time and schedule it. The choice is ours, as so poetically explained by my son, we either find the time for rest ourselves or God will give us that time. Rest and be still, schedule your "me time" today for the week. Find your Sabbath and be prepared for the healing power.

If we could all be children, then we would have no responsibilities right? You are a child, a child of God **always.** Play, work, and remember yourself or you make become "Jack!" Do you remember the *Shining*?

The Taste of Egypt

∽

It was late one evening as I laid in bed thinking about that night's devotions: The Israelites Escape from Egypt. I laid there asking God what I was to learn from this story. I mean, I was already under the belief that God takes care of His people and has set us free, what more could I learn? I mean let's face it; most of us are not slaves to an evil ancient empire.

> "Therefore, say to the Israelites: 'I am the Lord, and I will bring you out from under the yoke of the Egyptians. I will free you from being slaves to them, and I will redeem you with an outstretched arm and with mighty acts of judgment. I will take you as my own people, and I will be your God. Then you will know that I am the Lord your God, who brought you out from under the yoke of the Egyptians. And I will bring you to the land I swore with uplifted hand to five to Abraham, to Isaac and to Jacob. I will give it to you as a possession. I am the Lord.'"
> Exodus 6: 6 – 8 (NIV)

At the time of this devotion, I was working as a fulltime field service computer engineer, I definitely did not feel like any Israelite in Egypt must have felt, within a week I was awaken to the story in a new light.

It was a typical Monday; I was driving the regular commuting route of so many of my neighbors. We each would leave our homes, drive the allotted hour to our daily post, where we fulfilled the obligation to earn our income to keep our homes. As the day dragged on and on, the headache grew and grew. Finally, the dreaded commute home, but then home would be the safe and relaxation place so desired by all. The drive was horrendous, it is always worse with a headache. Stop and go, go and stop, continued for over the allotted hour, time is fast as an adult, almost like fleeting as a blink of an eye. I made it, the drive to my condo, so far I had traveled just to be able to prompt my feet up and relax.

Here was the spot, right next to my dogs, sitting and watching a little TV before bed. I could hear the plague in the other room, the pager sounding off for me to respond. Funny, never considered the pager a plague until that moment. I brushed off the thought and responded to the page. I drove through most of the night. It took the rest of the night to get the system up and running. The head was pounding beyond imagine. I left for the truck; a quick nap will do me good. It seemed like five minutes, when the car phone rang. Technology is a curse I thought. Again, an interesting conclusion and again I brushed the thought off. I had another call; Tuesday was not going to be any better than Monday.

I rushed to the other side of the state and began the repairs there. I finished with just enough time to fight the traffic back to the office and back home, yippee rush hour.

Wednesday was meeting day at the office, a justification of each department for their budget. The discussions were becoming more and more difficult with sales continuing to give service a way. There was the build relationship thought, but if you give the milk away for free who buys the cow arguments. There seemed to be no compromise and no solution, one pulled one way and another pulling the other. The strategies for each were in different corners. A great speaker and communicator I have never given much thought as a true characteristic of myself. Here I was put in the position to lead and communicate our goals with the partnership of a group that was in a different corner.

Wednesday evening's devotion was the part with Moses discussing with God how he was not a good speaker. I started laughing through the devotions, probably loosing more focus than I should have, but I could not help but begin to sense the understanding of this story in my life.

Thursday and Friday were more late night service calls, it really was wrong in my mind of customers to work on a system all day, and call just before the daily contract hours expired, expecting free services. As I sat in church on Sunday, listening to the sermon, and given the opportunity, rushing to the Alter to discuss the strength I was in need of.

This had been a repeated prayer request to God over the past several months, strength to be a field service engineer with the added pressure of administration. It had seemed for months my prayers had gone unanswered. Every day I go home with a headache, and every morning I dread the day ahead. It was funny how a career that I had once enjoyed had become such a burden, or as it came to me at the Alter, how I had become such a slave to my career. It was time to move on; I would have enough strength to fulfill my obligations for six months.

On Monday, I went into work, walked into my supervisor's office, and explained that I would be resigning in six months. Every day the thought that I might have misunderstood the Alter calling; I was reminded with "the Taste of Egypt."

The taste of Egypt is God's way of assisting us with moving on in our lives. Have you ever been in the moments that it was horrible, a point you never want to go back to? That is what the story of the Israelites and the taste of Egypt are all about. If the place you are leaving is wrong and dreaded the place you are going can only be right and brighter.

> In the desert the whole community grumbled against
> Moses and Aaron. The Israelites said to them, "If only
> we had died by the Lord's hand in Egypt! There we sat

around pots of meat and ate all the food we wanted, but
you have brought us out into this desert to starve this
entire assembly to death."

Then the Lord said to Moses, "I will rain down bread
from heave for you. The people are to go out each day and
gather enough for that day. In this way I will test them
and see whether they will follow my instructions."

Exodus 16: 2 – 4 (NIV)

The day I resigned, I returned to my cubical to receive a long awaited
call, my lawsuit had been settled from my car accident, and I would be
able to return to college to change my career. It was manna from heaven.
I could not help but believe that this was the path that God had placed
me. I realize that not all of us receive the gift of a lawsuit to fall back on,
but we must believe that we are going to receive manna and quail in the
desert; He does not send us where He has not already gone.

Trust me, when I entered college again as an adult with all those
youth, I felt the fear rise. Fortunately, I had moved onto a new devotion:
Joshua. Through every test and late night typing assignment, this was
constant: "Have I not commanded you? Be strong and courageous. Do
not be terrified; do not be discouraged, for the Lord your God will be
with you wherever you go." Joshua 1: 9(NIV)

I have given this advice to some of my friends. They have been honest
to explain their situations, and as we discuss them, it becomes apparent
that they are receiving the taste of Egypt. The calling to move forward
to not stay in the comfortable because it is known, but the willingness to
walk out in faith realizing that you know not where the manna will fall,
but it will fall from God.

Scientist and historians argue today to prove whether the Israelites
were ever captives and slaves in Egypt, hoping to discourage our faith in

the Bible. It is my argument that whether a people were slave in ancient times does not dismiss the message of the story to us in our time. We are all slaves to something, whether it is a career, social standings, good vice or bad. We all call on God regularly to give us strength to fight the same battles over and over daily. The definition of insanity is to do the same thing over and over expecting a different outcome. So take a leap of faith, make a change in your path at night, follow the fiery cloud through the desert, the promise land is worth each step.

The taste of Egypt comes in a swift movement by God. One day, you are going along on your path, and something about the path has injured you. You get plagued by constant nagging. You are praying for deliverance, you just cannot take another load of the day. Your taste of Egypt nags until the day, God frees you. Your life changes in the night, you no longer head down the same path. You follow the cloud of doubt, wondering in the desert not sure of where you are. You want to turn back, back to the known and feel comfortable, but the path is not there. The river has flooded back across; there is no way to return from whence you came.

The taste of Egypt comes to you in the form of an unthinking comment from another person or child. The voice that says you are heading in the right direction. You are no longer stressed with the decisions of the day; you feel relief in realizing that the deliverance is around the corner. The taste of Egypt with all its fears brings you peace and understanding.

Ask yourself, what is the point of the story today? God made His book universal to time, so what are you a slave to? Being a slave means there is hope for escape on your own. Ask yourself, what keeps the thorn in your side, what keeps popping up, prompting you to leave? What are your plagues? Don't you see your burning bush? Can't you hear the voice calling you to freedom?

That's a Covet

I t was early in my childhood that I memorized Psalms 23. It often pops into my head at the strangest times. However, while I was unemployed I was struck by it's haunting almost daily.

The week had been long, staying home with many channels on the television but nothing to watch. There were no real nibbles on my resume and I was starting to become claustrophobic. I am not the type of person that sits very well remember I am a work-a-holic. I could honestly start to understand how the animals in animal shelters must feel. Talk about my own *Shining*.

I was meditating in bed, just lying still, allowing my mind and heart to find each other and be at peace. I was almost completely through my thoughts before they hit me.

> Surely goodness and love will follow me all the days of my life, and I will dwell in the house of the Lord forever. You prepare a table before me in the presence of my enemies. You anoint my head with oil; my cup overflows. Even though I walk through the valley of the shadow of death, I will fear no evil, for you are with me; your rod and your staff, they comfort me. He makes me lie down in green pastures, he leads me beside quiet waters, he restores my soul. He guides me in the paths of righteousness for his name's sake. The Lord is my shepherd. I shall not be in want. Psalms 23: 6 – 1 (NIV)

I listened to the silent chant in my head, and then it hit me. I was reciting Psalms 23 backwards. After laughing for a minute, thinking that this exercise would be a cool road test, similar to the DUI test police use, recite the alphabet backwards. You know on the spiritual highway, would it not be great if there were little police angels going around testing your knowledge. Pass this test and continue on your way, your path is correct.

I, of course, in my normal sarcasm, replied to God, "No, I don't want, I NEED a job!"

David stated it very clearly. We are provided the need of a place to rest; He leads me beside quiet waters. Our need for food, taken care of, He prepares a table before me in the presence of my enemies. The need for protection, I will fear no evil, for He is with me; His rod and staff, they comfort me.

So in the stillness of my meditation I hear, "Do you have a place to sleep?" Of course, I do, I am lying in bed and realize that it would still be there tomorrow "Did you eat dinner tonight before you came to bed?" Of course, I did, and there is still food for future days. "Then why sarcastic?"

I NEED a job. Need an interesting word: A condition requiring relief, a necessity, something necessary but lacking.

The next morning and virtually all day that Saturday I heard from my son all his needs. He needed a new Lego. He needed a new basketball goal. He needed a new jersey. I tried to explain to him the difference of want and need, but was having no luck, only turning into a "bad" parent: Opps, starting to sound like me and my thoughts last night.

I have read Psalms 23 so many times, which it scrolls through my mind in reverse order, why? I have a psychology degree so I have studied Maslow's hierarchy of needs pyramid so much it too envelopes my thoughts. Again in my bent way of thinking, God provided Maslow with the answers in Psalms 23. He takes care of the shelter, food, protection, and eliminates the fears. The first verse is crucial.

The Lord is my shepherd, and I shall not be in want. If everything else is taken care of, in the manner that shepherds take care of their sheep, then everything else in my wishes is a want, a covent. I wanted a job for the sanity of my mind not for the need of provisions. Consider this; unemployment requires one to be still, to depend deeply on faith.

Employment provides noise, distractions to life, and busy time. Unemployment provides peace, silence, and stillness. In evitable, I needed to be still and be quiet. I needed to be dependent. I needed to relax and let the shepherd find me.

In my rush to do His work, I lost sight of Him. I would run out the door daily to get to work. I would scurry through the entire daily task, not finding much me time in the rush of the days. You remember the old saying "A week without prayer, makes one weak." I was there.

I faced each day as though it was the valley of death. My spirit was being drained and I had no time to go to the still waters for replenishing. The quiet time was only on vacation and breaks. The cup would get overflowing and then drain after a few days of work.

Who stated we were required to have careers or jobs? Who made these a need instead of a want? Jesus was a carpenter, but yet, we never read of him working on any houses or buildings. He was teaching not working. He needed food, it was there.

So how do you get from work to service?

A man can do nothing better than to eat and drink and find satisfaction in his work. This too, I see, is from the hand of God, for without him, who can eat or find employment? To the man who pleases him, God gives wisdom, knowledge and happiness, but to the sinner

he gives the tasks of gathering and storing up wealth to
hand it over to the one who pleases God. Ecclesiastes 2:
24 – 26 a (NIV)

The Lord is my shepherd; I shall not be in want. I had to change my
praise and pray from asking for a job, to asking for a place for my talents
to be in service to God. The first step out on the walk of faith is to find
something else to do with your time besides sitting on the couch.

Take the moment you have been given to go to the morning Bible
study. Take the moment to watch your child grow. Take the moment to
rest and be at peace. God takes care of the sparrow and you are greater
to Him than a bird. His time is unknown, scientist and religious people
have argued the seven day creation for many years, and the point is that
everything was completed on time. David was rescued from Saul at the
right time. The angel appeared in the firing furnace right when the three
needed them. God comes at His time, and believe it or not that time will
be appropriate. Trust in Him and build faith.

As you are unemployed and you wish you could go with the others
off to their daily duties, note whether you are coveting them or are you
serving Him?

Take heart and remember during your meditation: "'Dear woman,
why do you involve me?' Jesus replied. 'My time has not yet come.'"
John 2: 4 (NIV) your time will come and your service will be great in
accordance to God's plan.

Peace I leave with you; my peace I give you. I do not
give to you as the world gives. Do not let your hearts be
troubled and do not be afraid. John 14: 27 (NIV)

Lucky as They Go

Life is not fair. Work on earth is all meaningless, at least if you watch some people. I have worked for many years and have noticed at every job interval, there has always been at least one person "hitting the lottery."

I had one co-worker that abused all the attendance policies we had. She would come to work later and later as the year's passed by, then she would leave earlier and earlier. It was often the joke on the team that surely it cost more in gas than the hours she was willing to work. To add insult to injury, one of the days that she had decided to come to work, she was rear-ended. She won a large settlement for the accident and was able to retire from our occupation.

I sit and look at her experience and question where I am and why? I felt much like the Psalmists.

> How long, O Lord? Will you forget me forever? How long will you hide your face from me? How long must I wrestle with my thoughts and every day have sorrow in my heart? How long will my enemy triumph over me? Psalm 13: 1 – 2 (NIV)

Not that she was my enemy, I realized my enemy to be much bigger than her, but the thoughts of here I am Lord doing good works and being left behind. I had quit a career that I was safe in and took the walk out in faith to serve God, and had struggled in the world every day since.

I try to be a happy person and be thankful for what I have and where

I am. But there are days when my thoughts wonder to disappointment. We as humans have the weakness of wanting to be important to have things that mark our success. When we see others who are not serving God and obtaining success, it makes it hard to not cry out like the Psalmist.

How do we get to the point that Christ has called us of acceptability?

> So when you give to the needy, do not announce it with trumpets, as the hypocrites do in the synagogues and on the streets, to be honored by men. I tell you the truth, they have received their reward in full. Matthew 6: 2 (NIV)

It is hard on Earth to keep your eyes fixed on heavenly rewards when struggling with employment and the inability to pay your bills. How do you remember that rewards are yet to come? How do you feel secure in what you are doing when you feel in prison?

I was working in an after school program, working with kids that society was giving up on. The program was little when I started; we barely accomplished getting homework complete. The program was incomplete, running for only a couple of days a week for each age group. It left many students behind.

I had been working the program for a few years, it had grown. Students were finding success and blossoming. The program had tripled in number of students attending, the teachers were impressed and promoting the program. Within the school building I was, the program was working.

Another program began and created issues in space, safety, and responsibility. As I fulfilled my duties of advocating for my students, I found myself up against a formable enemy. I had gone to battle, unknowingly, against one of the highest powers in the school corporation. I was dismissed immediately.

I have spent several weeks pondering what had happened. I have prayed several times, why this has happened. How can someone doing God's work and doing a good job at service, find them outside looking in?

As time continued to pass and my enemies continued to be rewarded for my efforts and I sit at home waiting for the phone to ring, I wonder how long?

Ironically, the person I was instructed to not rehire at the beginning year was the person administration relied upon to take my position.

It is true every day you wrestle with your thoughts, thoughts that soon become enemies as well. There were days when I was convinced that I had walked out of God's plan. There were moments when I could not even generate a pray for assistance only questioning: What did I do wrong.

The sorrow in my heart was not only from letting the kids and teachers down, but for letting God down. As I said, soon the thoughts become your enemy. I attempted to reassure myself. I surrounded myself with music to calm the storm inside of me, but still in the fear, pain, and rage and I cried out: How long?

Your misery is anointed with alcohol when you hear of someone so under deserving wins the lottery. The person not only does not share with friends and family and work to get out of debt, the person goes to Las Vegas with some friends. The luck keeps falling on the "fortunate." Right?

To halt the thoughts one has to find focus, one has to find refuge and what better refuge in the solace of: "they have received their reward in full."

By trusting in the words of Jesus, you get through the haunting thoughts of your mind.

This is the time that faith is built. The time when you look at your deeds and realize that you did your best and that you have followed His commands. This is the time you appreciate being His.

Studies have demonstrated that people who attend church are least likely to have depression during major chaotic times in their lives. How can Christians get depressed with God in their back pocket? A friend even noted to me, most people get depressed, overweight and pick up bad habits during these times, but not you.

You have problems, you turn to God and the problems become little pebbles to be kicked to the side. You have fear, you turn to God and the fear is calmed much like a storm. You have a bad day, you turn to God and scream how long and He answers your call.

Some people may be lucky. They may get a way with being "slow walkers," not pulling their own weight at work. They may even spend money as if pulling off a paper towel from the roller, but their luck is limited.

I would much rather like keeping God in my back pocket, than be lucky. I appreciate a God who allows me to cry out, counts the tears, wipes the tears, and prepares the solution. It is difficult to get upset and jealous over the rewards of others, when I know that my God has noticed me and is taking note.

I played basketball for many years. I made a lot of shots. I remember one game I made that half court shot at half time. Cool, we should be fired up to come back. Wrong! The half court shot I took would be the last made bucket of the night for me. I was lucky with that shot. Half time was cool, but the end of the game was not.

Remember, lucky as they go, but only here.

No Home for Nomads

Have you ever noticed that most of the "famous" characters of the Bible do not have a home? Noah had an ark that drifted. Abraham and most of his descendants were nomads. Jesus, the disciples, and the apostles, all had no home ownership. Why?

Some people use the argument that they have no homes because a home ties a person to a loan. It limits our ability to freely follow God's calling. It causes us to put our oath on a piece of paper, much becoming a slave to our banks.

Others have theorized that home ownership is wrong because we do not belong here. We are "aliens" to this place. We are "hanging out" waiting on the second calling of Jesus to our homes.

Both of these are great reasons behind why we should not seek the desire to own a home. However, if we consider that we are not to build a home based on the concern of division, and then we can move to more openness.

> The Lord had said to Abram, "Leave your country, your people and your father's household and go to the land I will show you." Genesis 12: 1 (NIV)

Abram, later to be called Abraham, was called from his house, from his people and from his country. God called him away from his homeland, why would God do this? What would be our lesson from this?

By leaving his land and his father's household, Abram became totally dependent upon God. He had to go where God commanded. He was dependent upon God for food and water. He found companionship in God.

Abram had to trust in God: A trust that most of us have not had to experience. By most of us the accepted definitions are: to have confidence or faith in someone, friends, family and God. Yet, it is also defined to allow without fear. Abram lived without fear to follow God; he did not just have faith or confidence, he had trust.

I remember when I left for my first career moving in Cincinnati. I would not only be living in a new town without any of my family or friends, but traveling regularly. There was fear racing out of every pore of my body. I was so unsure of where I was and what I was to be doing. I mean what if I fail.

The first night in the apartment was the worst. I could hear every sound of the city. It was hard to figure out if the sounds were outside or inside.

After being a wake for hours, I finally put myself to rest by allowing myself to hear the calming. I rested because I felt the comforting that I had been called to this place.

What was the moving to new location teaching me? I had to learn trust and accept companionship. Funny when you are growing up with the same people in all your classes, you tend to grow into friendships. This is the same with God. You have to grow in trust with Him.

When I started my new career I was mad at God. Every turn I had taken to that point had been a huge obstacle. Doors were slammed in my face at every turn. I had a scholarship to college lost on a knee injury. I went into the Air Force and was promptly dismissed because I had had knee surgery. My parents made too much money so I could not get any financial assistance for college.

As I have stated above, I believed I was a person on my own path. But the path was leading me to God; I was just a slow learner to this fact. The first lesson was that first month. I had to fully **rel**y **on G**od, be a FROG. I had to trust God every night I went to sleep in the strange apartment or in a strange motel. I had to trust God with every encounter, even if I was not directly asking Him for protection.

There were so many times that my expense checks were larger than my payroll checks. Trust in all things, just like Abram.

I was traveling back from a job site with my supervisor in the car with me when I noticed that we were getting really low on fuel. Amazingly here in my rear view mirror is the image of a friend.

The chances of a friend passing me on the highway from one service call and me about to run out of gas seemed like a miracle. I felt the relief coming over me, but then she drove on by just waving her hand.

The only device that I had at my resource was trust. I had to trust that God would get us back to the office. I had to trust that God would get me to the bank before it closed with my expense check. Expense checks are live checks not directly deposited. I had to have trust that I would then get to the gas station. Trust not just faith.

So how are faith and trust different? Faith is belief in a supernatural power or a power that controls human destiny. Faith believes that I would be safe on the trip. Faith in the power of God would not fill up the fuel tank.

As a matter of point, faith would have been fulfilled by my friend pulling over and giving me a few dollars for gas. God would have demonstrated great power over human destiny by providing cash on the side of an interstate.

Trust is more than faith. Think of the exercise where one person falls back into the arms of another to build trust between groups of people. This is what driving down an interstate without gas is like, falling into the arms of God.

When we pack up our bags and refuse to buy the house, be a nomad, we learn the real trust that Abram had. We learn to live without fear. Imagine for a moment if you allow yourself in all aspects of your life to live without fear.

> But seek first his kingdom and his righteousness, and all these things will be given to you as well. Therefore do not worry about tomorrow, for tomorrow will worry about itself. Each day has enough trouble of its own. Matthew 6: 33 (NIV)

No home ownership means no mortgage payments to be tied to; being a nomad brings real trust in God and a companionship. As Jesus taught us, being a nomad is seeking first the kingdom of God and not worrying about tomorrow.

My son has had an admiration for "hobos" of history. The people who road the rails going from one place to the next, when asked why, he thought it was remarkable that they were happy without a home.

Could you imagine finding happiness by not having a home and being a nomad? God has.

Which Leader should we choose?

As I sat in a political science class, the professor started stating all the people that proposition the government daily. All these various groups represent us and many of the groups overlap each other and often times opposing each other. There is also the obvious that I do not always agree with everything that each of these organizations protest.

Presidents, congressional representatives, senators, kings, queens and prime ministers have the duties of protecting the nations against each other, and not the sight to view the people.

Even though, our leaders are here to serve the people, the ones who elected them. This is a failure in the system. This is probably why God warned us against organized government.

> Samuel told all the words of the Lord to the people who were asking him for a king. He said, "This is what the king who will reign over you will do: He will take your sons and make them serve with his chariots and horses, and they will run in front of his chariots. Some he will assign to be commanders of thousands and commanders of fifties, and others to plow his ground and reap his harvest, and still others to make weapons of war and equipment for his chariots. He will take your daughters to be perfumers and cooks and bakers. He will take the best of your fields and vineyards and olive groves and give them to his attendants. He will take a tenth of your grain and of your vintage and give it to his officials and

attendants. Your menservants and maidservants and the best of cattle and donkeys he will take for his own use. He will take a tenth of your flocks, and you yourselves will become slaves." 1 Samuel 8: 10 – 17 (NIV)

The Israelites had some forty-four kings from Saul to Zedekiah. Throughout their atrocious times, they only had a handful of kings that were concerned about the community and its relationship with God. Many of the kings mislead the group and created more problems in the people's lives than they could have imagined.

Every election we hear promises from those asking for our votes. At each stop, the politicians change their speeches to please the crowd. If they are in a hunting society, they push for everyone to own guns and less gun control. If they are in an education society, they are pushing for more funding for education and more support for the schools with at risk students.

Ironically, once in office, the promises are forgotten. We the people vote in office those officials we want to change the country by laws. Laws that forbid behavior, laws which take away free will, the one thing God has never taken.

We look to our government for changes in our society and not to ourselves and to our God. We expect laws to govern people's behavior all the while taking our eyes off the real leader. We expect our governments to provide the necessities promised by God.

We want our elders to be taken care of in health and living. We want our children to have a future with promising educations. We want to not see the poor on the streets starving, especially kids.

People complain of welfare or workfare, but yet, it was a part of God's original plan for community.

When you reap the harvest of your land, do not reap to
the very edges of your field or gather the gleanings of
your harvest. Do not go over your vineyard a second time
or pick up the grapes that have fallen. Leave them for the
poor and the alien, I am the Lord your God. Leviticus
19: 9 – 10 (NIV)

If we were to set our eyes upon the real leader of a community of
people, then we would be less disappointed. Each year after a politician is
in office, his or her status usually declines based on observed performances.
A person cannot satisfy all those supporters.

Back to why God did not want to give Israel a king, He wanted to
be the King of them. Read the laws of God, understanding that He was
building a nation, you will find the laws are better than any kingdom's
or nation's constitutions.

The Ten Commandments could be broken into two categories: First,
those which apply to serving God in total service; and Second, those
which apply to living in a community.

I am saying that we have now established our interactions that we
require superficial leaders, pawns in the network of humanity. I am not
saying that our leaders have not sought the insight and wisdom of God
before making crucial decisions. I am saying though that we have chosen
the easy way out of problems.

We complain about the systems that have been established. We divide
ourselves over laws that eliminate free will. I agree there are some laws
that we need because there are those of us who see no speed as too fast.
The laws attempting to eliminate people's choices for a safer community
are where our leaders mislead us much as those from Israel.

But if serving the Lord seems undesirable to you, then

> choose for yourselves this day whom you will serve, whether the gods your forefathers served beyond the River, or the gods of the Amorites, in whose land you are living. Joshua 24:15 (NIV)

God gave an open invitation for our behaviors to destroy each other or to lift each other up. After guiding the Israelites from captivity in Egypt, through the desert, and through many battles to settle in the land He had promised them, He gave them the choice as to serve Him or not: to obey His laws or turn away.

At the very individual level, we cannot request from our governments what our God can do. The next time you are in a political discussion concerning how a certain politician has mislead our nation, challenge the conversation on what have we done. What point have we rolled up ourselves to help someone out? What afternoon did we go and volunteer as a tutor? When did you pick up a stranger on the corner and take her/him to dinner?

The government is for the government, the people are for the people. God gave us free will, why would we want the government to take this away? We only create more problems in our society when we create rules to direct individual behavior.

If governments are so great for society, then why did one crucify our Lord and Savior?